# ACKNOWLEDGMENTS

SPECIAL THANKS TO THOSE WHO MADE SIGNIFICANT CONTRIBUTIONS TO THE BOOK.

MY SON, BRYAN YUSKIW FOR HAND-PRINTING THE BOOK AND MAKING IT ALL POSSIBLE.

MARGO EMBURY, THE PUBLISHING CONSULTANT FOR CENTAX OF CANADA. YOUR ENTHUSIASM, ENERGY, EXPERTISE AND ASSISTANCE WAS TRULY OUTSTANDING. THANKS AGAIN MARGO!

PETER BOLLI FOR HIS GENIUS WITH A CAMERA. GREAT SHOTS PETER!

THANKS TO ROB SPLANE AND CHRISTINE ROSEWARN FOR THEIR SUPPORT AND ASSISTANCE ON THE COVER DESIGN.

ALL OUR FRIENDS AND RELATIVES FOR PROMOTIONAL ASSISTANCE.

LEONARD ZENITH FOR HIS LEGAL SERVICES.

JERRY SNUKAL FOR HIS ACCOUNTING SERVICES.

ALSO THE SOUTHPORT BRANCH, BANK OF COMMERCE FOR THEIR FINANCIAL SUPPORT.

THIS COOKBOOK TOOK
1½ YEARS TO COMPLETE,
ALTHOUGH IT'S NOT PERFECT
WE ARE CONFIDENT WE ALL
DID OUR BEST TO PROVIDE
SOMETHING FOR EVERYONE.

AUTHOR'S NOTE

P.S.
IF YOU HAPPEN TO COME
ACROSS A MISTAKE DON'T BE
ALARMED, AS WE HAVE PROVIDED
SOMETHING FOR THOSE WHO
LOOK FOR FAULT IN EVERYTHING.

# DEDICATION

THIS COOKBOOK IS DEDICATED TO MY HUSBAND, FAMILY AND FRIENDS. THEIR SUPPORT AND ENCOURAGEMENT WAS GREATLY APPRECIATED.

DISHES AND ACCESSORIES COURTESY OF :

ANN KRUPNIK
CHEONG LUNG GROCERIES
GIFT GROVE - SOUTH CENTER
GUENTHER'S MOBILIA

# TABLE OF CONTENTS

# NOTES

# APPETIZERS

# CAMBODIAN SHISH KEBABS

2 LBS.      SIRLOIN
2 LBS.      CHICKEN BREASTS
1 TBSP.    CURRY POWDER
PINCH OF  CRUSHED RED CHILI PEPPER
1/2 CUP   VEGETABLE OIL
1/2 CUP   SOY SAUCE
3 CLOVES GARLIC, CRUSHED
1 1/2 TBSP. SUGAR
1/8 TSP.   SALT
1 TBSP.    TERIYAKI SAUCE
1 1/2 TSP. GRATED FRESH GINGER
1 CUP      GROUND, ROASTED,
              UNSALTED PEANUTS
1             GREEN PEPPER,
              CUT IN 1" SQUARES
1             LARGE ONION,
              CUT IN 1" PIECES,
              LAYERS SEPARATED
1 LB.       MUSHROOMS

CONTINUED

CUT MEAT INTO VERY THIN 3" STRIPS. STIR TOGETHER, CURRY, CHILI, OIL, SOY SAUCE, GARLIC, SUGAR, SALT, TERIYAKI AND GINGER IN A MEDIUM BOWL. SUBMERGE MEAT IN MARINADE, COVER AND REFRIGERATE OVERNIGHT. SOAK BAMBOO SKEWERS IN WATER FOR 30 MINUTES. ADD PEANUTS TO MEAT SAUCE, MIX WELL, ADD PEPPERS, ONIONS AND MUSHROOMS; STIR GENTLY TO COAT WITH SAUCE. SKEWER MEAT ON BAMBOO STICKS USING ONION, PEPPER OR MUSHROOM BETWEEN PIECES, AND DRIZZLE WITH REMAINING MARINADE. BROIL OR BARBEQUE OVER HIGH HEAT FOR ONLY A FEW MINUTES ON EACH SIDE UNTIL MEAT IS WELL BROWNED.

NOTE : ALL COOKING TEMPERATURES ARE IN FARENHEIT DEGREES.

SERVES 15-20

# Stuffed Mushroom Caps

```
12         LARGE MUSHROOMS
2 TBSP.    LEMON JUICE
1 TBSP.    PEANUT OIL
7 OZ       CRAB MEAT
1 CUP      CHOPPED WATER CHESTNUTS
1 TBSP.    DRY BREAD CRUMBS
1 TBSP.    CHOPPED GREEN ONION
1 TBSP.    LEMON JUICE
1 TBSP.    MINCED PARSLEY
1 TBSP.    SOY SAUCE
1          EGG, WELL BEATEN
```

WIPE MUSHROOMS WITH DAMP PAPER TOWEL TO CLEAN, REMOVE STEMS. TOSS CAPS IN LEMON JUICE, SET ASIDE. CHOP STEMS, FRY IN HOT OIL A MINUTE, REMOVE FROM HEAT, ADD REMAINING INGREDIENTS AND MIX WELL TO BLEND. STUFF CAPS AND PLACE IN SMALL SHALLOW PAN. BAKE AT 350° FOR 20 MINUTES, SERVE HOT. RECIPE SUGGESTED BY BETTY KRUMPITZ, WETASKIWIN, ALBERTA.

SERVES 4-6

# RUMAKI

| | |
|---|---|
| 1/3 CUP | SOY SAUCE |
| 1/4 TSP. | GROUND GINGER |
| 1/4 TSP. | CURRY POWDER |
| 1/2 LB. | CHICKEN LIVERS |
| 1 LB. | BACON, CUT INTO THIRDS |
| 1 CAN | WATER CHESTNUTS |

COMBINE SOY SAUCE, GINGER, AND CURRY POWDER IN A BOWL. CUT CHICKEN LIVERS IN THIRDS, AND ADD TO MARINADE FOR 4 HOURS. REMOVE AND DRAIN. ADD A THIN SLICE OF WATER CHESTNUT FOR EACH PIECE OF LIVER, WRAP IN BACON, AND SECURE WITH A TOOTHPICK. PLACE ON BROILING PAN, AND BROIL APPROXIMATELY 5 MINUTES. TURN A FEW TIMES SO BACON IS COOKED AND CRISP.

SERVES 6

13

# Appetizer Cheesecake

2½ CUPS CHEESE RITZ CRACKERS
2 CUPS SOUR CREAM
½ CUP GREEN OLIVES
1 GREEN PEPPER CHOPPED
1 SMALL ONION, CHOPPED
2 TBSP. LEMON JUICE
1 TSP. SALT
2 DROPS TABASCO
1 TSP. WORCESTERSHIRE SAUCE
¼ TSP. PAPRIKA
1 STALK CELERY, CHOPPED
1 HEAD ENDIVE OR LEAF LETTUCE
6 STUFFED OLIVES
PARSLEY SPRIGS
1 ORANGE SLICED VERY THIN.

CONTINUED...

USE A 9" SPRINGFORM PAN;
BRUSH WELL WITH MELTED BUTTER.
CRUSH CHEESE RITZ TO FINE CRUMBS,
THEN LAYER HALF ON BOTTOM OF
PAN. PUT SOUR CREAM, OLIVES,
GREEN PEPPER, ONION, LEMON JUICE,
SALT, TABASCO, WORCESTERSHIRE,
PAPRIKA AND CELERY IN BLENDER.
SET ON LOW SPEED UNTIL ALL ARE
FINELY CHOPPED. SPREAD OVER
CRUMB BASE AND SPRINKLE
REMAINING CRUMBS OVER TOP.
COVER WITH WAX PAPER AND
REFRIGERATE FOR 24 HOURS.
REMOVE SIDES FROM PAN, SET CAKE
ON SERVING DISH. DECORATE WITH
SLICED OLIVES ON TOP, WITH SPRIGS
OF PARSLEY, AND A FEW LEAVES
OF ENDIVE WITH ORANGE SLICES
AROUND THE SIDES.

SERVES 8

# Olive Cheese Balls

| | |
|---|---|
| 1/4 CUP | BUTTER |
| 1/2 CUP | FLOUR |
| 1/2 TSP. | PAPRIKA |
| 1/4 TSP. | SALT |
| 1 CUP | SHREDDED OLD CHEDDAR CHEESE |
| 8 OZ JAR | STUFFED OLIVES, DRAINED |

BLEND BUTTER, FLOUR, PAPRIKA, SALT AND CHEESE UNTIL WELL MIXED. SHAPE INTO SMALL BALLS, FLATTEN, THEN SHAPE AROUND OLIVE. ROLL GENTLY IN PALM OF HANDS TO MAKE SMOOTH. PLACE ON COOKIE SHEET, AND INTO OVEN AT 425° UNTIL WARMED THROUGH, ABOUT 15 MINUTES.

SERVES 10-12

# KAUIA CHICKEN WINGS

20        CHICKEN WINGS
1 CUP    CORN SYRUP
2 TBSP.  MAZOLA OIL
2 TBSP.  PINEAPPLE JUICE
1 TBSP.  GRATED FRESH GINGER
4 CLOVES GARLIC CRUSHED

    WASH WINGS, CUT AT JOINTS
AND REMOVE TIPS. PUT WINGS IN
A LARGE BAKING PAN. COMBINE
THE REMAINING INGREDIENTS, MIX
WELL, THEN POUR OVER WINGS.
COVER AND SET IN REFRIGERATOR
TO MARINATE ABOUT 4 HOURS,
MIXING OCCASIONALLY. PREHEAT
OVEN AT 350°. REMOVE WINGS
FROM MARINADE, PLACE ON RACK
WITH A LARGE COOKIE SHEET, AND
COOK ABOUT 50 MINUTES UNTIL
TENDER, TURNING TO BROWN
BOTH SIDES.

SERVES  8-10

# Shrimp Cocktail

| | | |
|---|---|---|
| 1 | QT. | WATER |
| 1 | TBSP. | COARSE SALT |
| 1 | | BAY LEAF |
| 1 | CUP | CHOPPED CELERY |
| ½ | TSP. | PICKLING SPICE |
| 1 | TBSP. | VINEGAR |
| 24 | | JUMBO SHRIMP |

BRING WATER TO BOIL WITH SALT, BAY LEAF, CELERY, SPICE AND VINEGAR. ADD SHRIMP, SIMMER 8 TO 10 MINUTES. DRAIN, PEEL OFF SHELLS, REMOVE BLACK VEIN AND CHILL. PREPARE SAUCE.

# Cocktail Sauce

| | | |
|---|---|---|
| 6 | TBSP. | CHILI SAUCE |
| 2 | TBSP. | LEMON JUICE |
| 1 | TBSP. | HORSERADISH |
| 1 | TSP. | WORCESTERSHIRE SAUCE |
| 2 | DROPS | TABASCO SAUCE |
| 1 | | GREEN ONION, FINELY CHOPPED |

COMBINE ALL INGREDIENTS, MIX AND CHILL. PLACE SAUCE ON BED OF LETTUCE, HANG SHRIMP AROUND RIM OF DISH.

SERVES 4

# Honey Garlic Spareribs

| | |
|---|---|
| 3 LBS. | PORK SPARERIBS |
| ½ CUP | SOY SAUCE |
| 3 TBSP. | BROWN SUGAR |
| 3 TBSP. | VINEGAR |
| ½ CUP | SHERRY |
| 3 | LARGE CLOVES OF GARLIC, CRUSHED |
| 1 TBSP. | CATSUP |
| 2 TBSP. | LIQUID HONEY |

TRIM EXCESS FAT, CUT INTO INDIVIDUAL SERVINGS, AND PLACE RIBS IN A LARGE BOWL. COMBINE NEXT 6 INGREDIENTS, AND USE TO MARINATE RIBS FOR 4 HOURS, MIXING 3 OR 4 TIMES. PREHEAT OVEN AT 325°, PLACE RIBS ON BROILER PAN AND BAKE APPROXIMATELY 1½ HOURS. TURN RIBS A FEW TIMES DURING BAKING AND BASTE WITH REMAINING MARINADE EVERY 20 MINUTES. MIX HONEY WITH 1 TSP. WATER AND BRUSH ON RIBS TO GLAZE FOR THE LAST 20 MINUTES OF BAKING.

SERVES 4-6

# Avocado Shrimp Mousse

```
1      ENVELOPE UNFLAVORED GELATIN
1/4 CUP  COLD WATER
2  LARGE AVOCADOS
3  TBSP. LEMON JUICE
1  TSP.  SALT
1/4 TSP.  PEPPER
4         GREEN ONIONS, FINELY CHOPPED
1/4 TSP.  CAYENNE
1/2 CUP   MAYONNAISE
1  CUP   WHIPPING CREAM
2  CUPS  CANNED SMALL SHRIMP
1/2 CUP   CANNED MEDIUM SHRIMP
```

SPRINKLE GELATIN OVER COLD WATER IN SMALL SAUCEPAN; HEAT UNTIL DISSOLVED. MASH AVOCADO, ADD LEMON JUICE, STIR IN SALT, PEPPER, ONION, CAYENNE, MAYONNAISE, AND DISSOLVED GELATIN. WHIP CREAM LIGHTLY; FOLD IN. MIX 1/2 OF CREAM MIXTURE WITH 2 CUPS SMALL SHRIMP. LINE A MEDIUM LOAF PAN WITH PLASTIC WRAP.

CONTINUED

SPOON 1/2 OF REMAINING CREAM MIXTURE INTO BOTTOM OF PAN, SMOOTH EVENLY, SPOON IN SHRIMP MIXTURE, THEN TOP WITH LAST OF THE CREAM MIXTURE. COVER AND REFRIGERATE 3 TO 4 HOURS. TO SERVE, UNMOLD ONTO SERVING PLATTER, GARNISH WITH LETTUCE LEAVES AND LEMON TWISTS. DECORATE TOP WITH MEDIUM SHRIMP AND A SPRINKLE OF FRESH PARSLEY FOR COLOUR. SERVE WITH CRACKERS OR AS A SALAD WITH A BUFFET LUNCHEON.

SERVES 10-12

# Meatballs

| | |
|---|---|
| 2 | SLICES OF BREAD |
| 1 CUP | MILK |
| ½ LB | BEEF |
| ½ LB | PORK |
| ½ LB | VEAL |
| 2 | EGGS |
| ¼ CUP | CHOPPED ONION |
| 1 TBSP. | BUTTER |
| 3 TBSP. | FINELY CHOPPED PARSLEY |
| 1 TSP. | LEMON JUICE |
| 1 TSP. | WORCESTERSHIRE SAUCE |
| ½ TSP. | GRATED LEMON RIND |
| 1 TSP. | SALT |
| ¼ TSP. | PAPRIKA |
| | CORNSTARCH FOR COATING |
| | OIL FOR DEEPFRYING |

CONTINUED

SOAK BREAD IN MILK TO COVER. GRIND MEAT VERY FINE, ADD EGGS. LIGHTLY FRY ONION IN BUTTER AND ADD TO MEAT. SQUEEZE LIQUID FROM BREAD, ADD BREAD AND REMAINING INGREDIENTS TO MEAT. MIX WELL, SHAPE INTO 1" BALLS (APPROXIMATELY 60), CHILL FOR 1 HOUR. HEAT OIL TO 375°, ROLL MEATBALLS IN CORNSTARCH, AND DEEP-FRY UNTIL THEY ARE GOLDEN BROWN AND RISE TO THE TOP. DRAIN ON PAPER TOWELS. SERVE ON COCKTAIL PICKS.

NOTE: MEATBALLS MAY BE FROZEN IN COVERED CONTAINERS. HEAT IN COVERED BAKING DISH AT 400° FOR 20 MINUTES. DELICIOUS IN SPAGHETTI SAUCE OR IN A SWEET AND SOUR SAUCE.

MAKES APPROXIMATELY
60 MEATBALLS

# Oysters On The Half Shell

24      OYSTERS
1       LEMON
        DASH OF PEPPER
        COCKTAIL SAUCE, PAGE 20

BUY ATLANTIC OYSTERS FOR SERVING RAW, AS PACIFIC OYSTERS ARE BITTER. SHELLS MUST BE TIGHTLY CLOSED. CHECK THEM BEFORE BUYING. SCRUB SHELLS THOROUGHLY WITH COLD WATER AND A BRUSH, THEN CHILL. TO OPEN, HOLD THE OYSTER FIRMLY IN ORDER TO PRY WITH AN OYSTER KNIFE. DON'T DRAIN OFF THE JUICE; LEAVE IT WITH THE OYSTER ON THE DEEP HALF OF SHELL. ARRANGE 6 ON A PLATE OVER ICE AND A BED OF LETTUCE. PLACE A SMALL GLASS DISH OF COCKTAIL SAUCE IN CENTER AND A LEMON WEDGE ON THE SIDE. I LIKE THEM WITH JUST A BIT OF LEMON JUICE AND A DASH OF PEPPER.

SERVES 4

# OYSTERS ROCKEFELLER

| 24 | FRESH ATLANTIC OYSTERS |
|---|---|
| 4 TSP. | FINELY CHOPPED ONION |
| 1 TBSP. | BUTTER |
| 12 OZ. | SPINACH |
| 1 TBSP. | PERNOD |
| | SALT |
| | PEPPER |
| 1 CUP | HOLLANDAISE SAUCE, PAGE 45 |
| 1 TBSP | PARMESAN CHEESE |
| 1 | LEMON |

SELECT 2 DOZEN OYSTERS IN SHELLS, REMOVE FROM SHELLS AND SAVE BOTTOM SHELL FOR SERVING. SAUTÉ ONION IN BUTTER, ADD THE SPINACH, PERNOD, SALT AND PEPPER TO TASTE. PLACE SPINACH ON SHELLS, TOP WITH AN OYSTER, COVER WITH HOLLANDAISE SAUCE. SPRINKLE WITH PARMESAN CHEESE. BAKE 10 TO 15 MINUTES IN 375° OVEN. SERVE WITH LEMON SLICES.

SERVES 4

# ESCARGOTS

15 OZ.    CAN ESCARGOTS (48)
1½ CUPS SOFT BUTTER
1 TSP.    SALT
⅛ TSP.   PEPPER
1 OR 2   CLOVES GARLIC, CRUSHED
¼ CUP    MINCED PARSLEY
               FRENCH LOAF
               ESCARGOTS SHELLS (48)

DRAIN AND RINSE SNAILS UNDER RUNNING WATER, DRY ON PAPER TOWEL. CREAM BUTTER, ADD SALT, PEPPER, GARLIC AND PARSLEY. MIX WELL AND CHILL. HEAT OVEN TO 450°. PUT A BIT OF BUTTER IN EACH SHELL, ADD 1 SNAIL, THEN TOP WITH BUTTER, SET UPRIGHT IN SNAIL DISHES. SLICE FRENCH LOAF THICKLY, AND USING REMAINING BUTTER, BUTTER EACH SLICE. WRAP IN FOIL. WARM IN OVEN 10 MINUTES. BAKE ESCARGOTS 5 MINUTES, THEY ARE READY TO SERVE HOT AND BUBBLING.

CONTINUED

I PREFER FRESH SNAILS WHEN AVAILABLE. PLACE IN A LARGE POT OF COLD WATER AND LEAVE 15 TO 20 MINUTES SO THE SNAILS CAN COME OUT OF THE SHELLS AND WASH THEMSELVES OFF. COOK ABOUT 5 MINUTES IN JUST ENOUGH LIGHTLY SALTED, BOILING WATER TO COVER. DRAIN AND RINSE IN COLD WATER, REMOVE FROM SHELL WITH A FORK AND PROCEED AS FOR CANNED.

NOTE: WATCH CLOSELY WHEN THE SNAILS ARE BATHING IN COLD WATER AS THEY CAN BE QUITE ACTIVE. IT ISN'T APPRECIATED BY GUESTS WHEN A YOUNGSTER RUNS IN TO SAY, "THE SNAILS ARE CRAWLING UP THE KITCHEN CURTAINS." IF IT HAPPENS POUR YOUR GUESTS AN EXTRA COCKTAIL, A DOUBLE FOR YOURSELF, ADD A BIT OF JUICY GOSSIP AND DELAY DINNER A HALF HOUR. IT HELPS.

SERVES 6

# Caviar Mousse

1  PKG.  UNFLAVOURED GELATIN
1/4 CUP   COLD WATER
EGG LAYER
4   HARD BOILED EGGS, FINELY CHOPPED
1/2 CUP  MAYONNAISE
1/4 CUP   FINELY MINCED FRESH PARSLEY
1   LARGE ONION, FINELY CHOPPED
1   DASH OF TABASCO
    SALT TO TASTE
    PEPPER TO TASTE
1   TBSP. DISSOLVED GELATIN
AVOCADO LAYER
2   MEDIUM RIPE AVOCADOS, MASHED
1   LARGE GREEN ONION, FINELY CHOPPED
2   TBSP. LEMON JUICE
2   TBSP. MAYONNAISE
1   DASH OF TABASCO
    SALT TO TASTE
    PEPPER TO TASTE
1   TBSP. DISSOLVED GELATIN
SOUR CREAM LAYER
1 CUP   SOUR CREAM
1/2 CUP   RED ONION, FINELY CHOPPED
2 TBSP. DISSOLVED GELATIN
            4 OZ. BLACK CAVIAR
            LEMON JUICE

            CONTINUED

LINE THE INSIDE OF AN 8" SPRINGFORM PAN WITH PLASTIC WRAP OR FOIL. MIX GELATIN WITH WATER, HEAT SLOWLY TO DISSOLVE. MIX INGREDIENTS FOR EGG LAYER AND SPREAD ON BOTTOM EVENLY. MIX AVOCADO LAYER AND CAREFULLY SPREAD OVER EGG LAYER. MIX SOUR CREAM, RED ONION, AND GELATIN TOGETHER AND SPREAD OVER AVOCADO LAYER, SMOOTHING EVENLY. COVER WITH PLASTIC WRAP AND REFRIGERATE OVER-NIGHT. JUST BEFORE SERVING, PLACE CAVIAR IN A FINE SIEVE, AND RINSE LIGHTLY UNDER RUNNING WATER, SPRINKLE WITH LEMON JUICE AND DRAIN. PLACE MOUSSE ON LARGE SERVING PLATE, SPRINKLE ON CAVIAR, AND DECORATE WITH LEMON TWISTS AND A FEW SPRIGS FRESH PARSLEY. SERVE WITH TINY SLICES OF RYE BREAD AND AN ASSORTMENT OF CRACKERS.

SERVES 15-20

# Beer Cheese Fondue

1 TBSP.   MELTED BUTTER
1½ TBSP. CORNSTARCH
½ TSP.   PAPRIKA
½ TSP.   DRY MUSTARD
1 CUP    BEER
1 LB.    OLD CHEDDAR CHEESE, GRATED
1 LOAF   FRENCH BREAD, 1½" CUBES

COMBINE IN A FONDUE POT OVER MEDIUM HEAT THE BUTTER, CORNSTARCH, PAPRIKA AND MUSTARD. ADD BEER; HEAT AND STIR UNTIL THICKENED. ADD CHEESE AND STIR UNTIL MELTED. SET HEAT ON LOW AND SERVE WITH A PLATE OF BREAD CUBES. GIVE EACH GUEST A LONG-HANDLED FORK AND LET THEM DO THEIR OWN DIPPING.

SERVES   4

# CRAB OR LOBSTER FONDUE

10 OZ. CAN  CREAM OF SHRIMP SOUP
1/4 CUP  LIGHT CREAM
1/2 CUP  GRATED CHEDDAR CHEESE
6 1/2 OZ  CRAB OR LOBSTER MEAT
1 TBSP. LEMON JUICE
1/8 TSP. PAPRIKA
1/8 TSP. WHITE PEPPER
2 TBSP. SHERRY

COMBINE SOUP WITH CREAM IN FONDUE POT. HEAT AND STIR OVER MEDIUM HEAT. ADD NEXT 5 INGREDIENTS, STIR AND HEAT TO SERVING TEMPERATURE. ADD SHERRY, STIR AND SERVE WITH CUBED FRENCH BREAD, SEE METHOD IN BEER CHEESE FONDUE PAGE 32

SERVES  4

# Beef, Shrimp, and Chicken Fondue

| | |
|---|---|
| 1 LB. | SIRLOIN STEAK |
| 1 LB. | WHOLE CHICKEN BREAST |
| 1 LB. | MEDIUM SHRIMP |
| 1 QT. | PEANUT OIL |
| 1 TSP. | SALT |
| | LETTUCE LEAVES |
| | PARSLEY SPRIGS |

DIPPING SAUCES – SEE FOLLOWING RECIPES

REMOVE FAT FROM STEAK, CUT INTO 1" CUBES, DRY ON PAPER TOWEL. CUBE CHICKEN BREAST IN 3/4" PIECES. SHELL AND DEVEIN SHRIMP, RINSE AND DRY. MAKE 3 ROWS WITH LETTUCE LEAVES ON SERVING PLATTER. ON FIRST ROW ARRANGE CHICKEN PIECES, ON NEXT BEEF, ON THIRD SHRIMP. DECORATE WITH PARSLEY SPRIGS. HEAT OIL TO 375° IN FRYER, ADD SALT TO PREVENT SPLATTERING. GUESTS PROVIDED WITH LONG-STEMMED FORKS MAY COOK THE MEAT TO THEIR DESIRED TASTES.

SERVES 6

# FONDUE SAUCES

### RED SEA SAUCE :
½ CUP    SOUR CREAM
2 TBSP. CHILI SAUCE
2 TSP.    HORSERADISH
3 DROPS TABASCO
        MIX TO BLEND AND CHILL.

### SESAME SEED DIP :
¼ CUP    SOY SAUCE
2 TBSP. SESAME SEEDS, TOASTED
1            EGG
1½ TBSP. HONEY
1¼ CUPS MAZOLA OIL
2  TSP. SESAME SEED OIL
½" CUBE FRESH GINGER, CRUSHED
        PUT FIRST 4 INGREDIENTS
IN BLENDER. SLOWLY ADD REMAINING
INGREDIENTS WHILE BLENDING ON
LOW.  MIX WELL AND SERVE.

### HOT MUSTARD SAUCE :
6 TBSP. BOILING WATER
2 TBSP. DRY HOT MUSTARD
2 TSP. OLIVE OIL
⅛ TSP. TUMERIC
½ TSP. SALT
MIX AND SERVE.

ANCHOVY MUSTARD SAUCE :
1 3/4 OZ   ANCHOVIES, DRAINED
1 TBSP.  MINCED PARSLEY
1 CLOVE GARLIC, CRUSHED
1/3 CUP  MAZOLA OIL
3 TBSP. HOT DRY MUSTARD
2 TBSP. CIDER VINEGAR
        PUT ANCHOVIES THROUGH
GARLIC PRESS, COMBINE WITH
REMAINING INGREDIENTS IN A JAR.
CHILL AND SHAKE BEFORE SERVING.

HORSERADISH SAUCE :
1 CUP   SOUR CREAM
1 TBSP. HORSERADISH
2 TBSP. FRESH CHIVES, MINCED
        BLEND AND CHILL BEFORE
SERVING.

COCKTAIL SAUCE :
        SEE PAGE 20 FOR METHOD.

TERIYAKI SAUCE :
1/2 CUP SOY SAUCE
1 TBSP. SUGAR
1 CLOVE GARLIC, CRUSHED
1 TSP.  FRESH GINGER, PUT THROUGH
           GARLIC PRESS
2 TBSP. SHERRY
        HEAT FIRST 4 INGREDIENTS,
SIMMER  5 MINUTES, ADD SHERRY
AND SERVE ,

☆   HOT SOY SAUCE :
1/2 CUP  SOY SAUCE
1/3 CUP  WATER
1/4 CUP  BROWN SUGAR
1 TSP.  FRESH GINGER, CRUSHED
1 TSP.  GRATED ONION
1 TSP.  CORNSTARCH
        BLEND  INGREDIENTS, BRING
TO A BOIL AND SERVE HOT.

   NOTE :   ANY  COMBINATION OF
4 SAUCES  WILL BE SUFFICIENT
FOR DIPPING THIS AMOUNT OF MEAT.

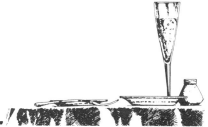

# Vegetable Dips

## BLUE CHEESE DIP:

3 TBSP. DRY VERMOUTH
2 TBSP. SOUR CREAM
4 OZ BLUE CHEESE, CRUMBLED
4 OZ CREAM CHEESE, CUBED

Put ingredients in blender, at medium speed until smooth. Cover and chill to blend flavors. Serve at room temperature.

## AVOCADO SHRIMP DIP:

2 RIPE AVOCADOS, PEELED AND PITTED
1 CUP SOUR CREAM
2 TBSP. CHILI SAUCE
½ TSP. SALT
4½ OZ DEVEINED SHRIMP

Blend avocado, sour cream, chili sauce, and salt on medium speed until smooth. Add shrimp; run only a minute just to chop shrimp. Chill and serve.

# Anchovy Canapes

4 OZ.     ANCHOVIES
1 SMALL ONION , CHOPPED
3 CLOVES GARLIC , CRUSHED
4 OZ.     CREAM CHEESE
2 TSP.   WORCESTERSHIRE SAUCE
3 TBSP. SOUR CREAM
         RYE BREAD, TOASTED, SQUARED
         PARSLEY SPRIGS FOR GARNISH

DRAIN ANCHOVIES, PUT IN BLENDER WITH NEXT 5 INGREDIENTS. BLEND UNTIL SMOOTH AND CHILL. SERVE AS A SPREAD ON THE TOAST, OR ON CRACKERS, AND TOP WITH A PARSLEY SPRIG. A TRAY OF CARROT AND CELERY STRIPS WILL ALSO BE EFFECTIVE FOR COLOR.

SERVES 4-6

41

# NOTES

# BREADS AND BRUNCHES

# Eggs Benedict

4       LARGE SLICES HAM
8            EGGS
4            ENGLISH MUFFINS
2            EGG YOLKS
½ CUP    BUTTER CUT INTO THIRDS
1            DASH OF SALT
1            DASH CAYENNE PEPPER
1 TBSP.  LEMON JUICE
2 TBSP.  SHERRY (CORBANS)

# Eggs Florentine

NOTE : USING COOKED SPINACH, PLACE
UNDER EGG TO MAKE EGGS FLORENTINE.

FRY HAM OVER LOW HEAT.
SPRAY EGG POACHER WITH MAZOLA
NO-STICK. BREAK 1 EGG INTO EACH
CUP, (I ADD THE WHITES FROM THE
2 YOLKS ALSO). ADD 1" WATER TO
TO POACHING PAN, COVER, COOK ON
MEDIUM HEAT. SLICE MUFFINS, TOAST
AND BUTTER. WHILE EVERYTHING IS
COOKING MAKE HOLLANDAISE SAUCE

SERVES 4

CONTINUED

# HOLLANDAISE SAUCE

PUT 1" WATER IN BOTTOM OF DOUBLE BOILER AND PLACE OVER MEDIUM HEAT. TO TOP ADD 2 EGG YOLKS AND 1 PIECE OF BUTTER, PLACE OVER HOT WATER AND HOLDING THE BUTTER WITH FORK TINES, STIR EGG YOLKS. WHEN BUTTER MELTS ADD NEXT PIECE, STIRRING THE SAME WAY, THEN THE THIRD PIECE. WITH A WOODEN SPOON STIR AND COOK A FEW MINUTES UNTIL THICKENED. REMOVE FROM HEAT, ADD SALT, CAYENNE, AND LEMON JUICE; BLEND. ADD SHERRY SLOWLY IN A STREAM STIRRING CONSTANTLY. NEVER LET THE WATER BOIL WHEN MAKING SAUCE AS THIS WILL CAUSE THE SAUCE TO CURDLE. IF THIS DOES HAPPEN, ADD A BIT OF COLD WATER AND WHISK VIGOROUSLY. TO SERVE, PLACE 2 MUFFIN HALVES ON EACH PLATE, 1 EGG ON EACH HALF, SPOON SAUCE OVER EGGS. ADD 1 SLICE OF HAM AND GARNISH WITH LETTUCE AND A SLICE OF TOMATO. (THIS IS A TERRIFIC BREAKFAST FOR CHRISTMAS MORNING)

# POTATO PANCAKES

| 3 CUPS | GROUND POTATOES |
|--------|-----------------|
| 1 | ONION , GRATED |
| 1 CLOVE | GARLIC |
| 2 | EGGS , SEPARATED |
| 1½ TBSP. | FLOUR |
| 1 TSP. | SALT |
| ⅛ TSP. | BAKING POWDER |
| | MARGARINE FOR FRYING |

PEEL LARGE POTATOES, CUT LENGTHWISE IN QUARTERS, COVER WITH COLD WATER, LET STAND 8 TO 12 HOURS, RINSE. PUT ONION, GARLIC, AND 1 PIECE OF POTATO THROUGH MEAT GRINDER, SET ASIDE. USE ANOTHER DISH AND GRIND REMAINING POTATOES, THEN DRAIN WELL AND ADD TO ONION AND GARLIC. ADD BEATEN EGG YOLKS, MIX LIGHTLY, THEN ADD FLOUR, SALT AND BAKING POWDER. WHIP EGG WHITES, BLEND IN LIGHTLY. FRY OVER MEDIUM HEAT UNTIL GOLDEN BROWN ON EACH SIDE. SERVE WITH PORK SAUSAGES.

SERVES 4

# MUSHROOM AND SEAFOOD CRÊPES

4          EGGS
½ TSP.     SALT
1¼ CUPS    FLOUR
1¾ CUPS    MILK
¼ CUP      MELTED BUTTER, COOLED

BEAT EGGS AND SALT TOGETHER, ADD REMAINING INGREDIENTS, BEAT UNTIL SMOOTH; THE BLENDER IS GREAT FOR THIS. LET BATTER STAND 1 HOUR, STIR AND COOK. USE A 5" FRYING PAN OVER MEDIUM HEAT, GREASE, ADD 2 TBSP. BATTER, TIP TO SPREAD QUICKLY. LIGHTLY BROWN ABOUT 2 MINUTES. YOU WILL NEED 16 CRÊPES ALTOGETHER.

# Mushroom Sauce

4 CUPS   CHICKEN STOCK
2 LBS.   FRESH MUSHROOMS
½ CUP    BUTTER
⅓ CUP    FLOUR
1 STALK  CELERY, CHOPPED
4 SPRIGS PARSLEY
½ TSP.   SALT
¼ TSP.   PEPPER
¼ TSP.   LEAF THYME
⅛ TSP.   NUTMEG
3        EGG YOLKS
⅓ CUP    WHIPPING CREAM

MAKE CHICKEN STOCK WITH
4 CUPS BOILING WATER AND 4 TSP.
CHICKEN SOUP BASE. CLEAN MUSHROOMS
AND REMOVE STEMS, SET CAPS ASIDE
FOR FILLING, CHOP STEMS FINELY. MELT
BUTTER IN A 1 QT. SAUCEPAN, SPRINKLE
IN FLOUR, STIRRING TO BLEND. REMOVE
FROM HEAT, STIR IN CHICKEN STOCK,
RETURN TO MEDIUM HEAT, COOK AND
STIR UNTIL BOILING.

CONTINUED

ADD MUSHROOM STEMS, CELERY, PARSLEY, SALT, PEPPER, THYME AND NUTMEG. BRING TO BOIL, THEN LET SIMMER 20 MINUTES UNCOVERED, STIRRING OFTEN. STRAIN MIXTURE SLOWLY, RETURN TO SAUCEPAN. BEAT EGG YOLKS, ADD CREAM, BLEND. SLOWLY ADD 1 CUP HOT SAUCE TO EGGS WHILE BEATING. THEN GENTLY POUR EGG MIXTURE INTO REMAINING SAUCE STIRRING CONSTANTLY. BRING JUST TO A BOIL AND REMOVE FROM HEAT.

## MUSHROOM FILLING:

|  | MUSHROOM CAPS (FROM SAUCE) |
|---|---|
| 1 CUP | WATER |
| 1/4 TSP. | SALT |
| 3 TBSP. | LEMON JUICE |

SLICE CAPS. BRING WATER AND SALT TO A BOIL. ADD LEMON JUICE AND MUSHROOMS. SIMMER 3 MINUTES, DRAIN. ADD 1/4 CUP SAUCE TO MUSHROOMS, BLEND LIGHTLY.

# Seafood Filling

1 LB.    SCALLOPS
1 CUP    BOILING WATER
2 TBSP.  LEMON JUICE
2 SPRIGS PARSLEY
1 SMALL ONION
3 TBSP.  BUTTER
1 CUP    CRAB MEAT
5 OZ.    LOBSTER
½ TSP.   SALT
¼ TSP.   PEPPER
2 TBSP.  SHERRY
2 HARD-BOILED EGGS, GRATED
2 TBSP.  PARMESAN CHEESE
         EXTRA PARMESAN CHEESE
    FOR SPRINKLING OVER CRÊPES.

      SIMMER SCALLOPS IN NEXT 4
INGREDIENTS FOR 5 MINUTES. DRAIN
AND QUARTER. HEAT BUTTER IN LARGE
SAUCEPAN, ADD SCALLOPS, CRAB,
LOBSTER, SALT AND PEPPER. COOK
GENTLY 2 MINUTES, STIRRING. REMOVE
FROM HEAT, STIR IN SHERRY, EGGS, AND
¼ CUP SAUCE, SET ASIDE.

CONTINUED

LIGHTLY GREASE 8 INDIVIDUAL BAKING DISHES, 6" LONG, OR USE A 13" x 9" BAKING PAN. STUFF EACH OF 8 CRÊPES WITH 1/3 CUP SEAFOOD FILLING, ROLL WITH SEAM SIDE DOWN, PLACE 1 IN EACH DISH. STUFF LAST 8 WITH 1/3 CUP MUSHROOM FILLING, ROLL AND SET BESIDE SEAFOOD CRÊPE. TO REMAING MUSHROOM SAUCE ADD 2 TBSP. PARMESAN CHEESE, BLEND. POUR SAUCE ENTIRELY OVER CRÊPES, SPRINKLE PARMESAN CHEESE LIGHTLY ON TOP. BAKE IN PREHEATED 450° OVEN UNTIL LIGHTLY BROWNED AND BUBBLING, ABOUT 10 MINUTES. SERVE IMMEDIATELY. IF YOU WISH TO MAKE THESE A DAY AHEAD, MAKE THE SAUCE AND FILLINGS COVER AND REFRIGERATE. THIS WILL ONLY LAST 1 NIGHT. FINISH PREPARATIONS DAY OF SERVING.

SERVES 8

51

# Roast Beef Sandwiches

| | |
|---|---|
| 1/4 LB. | BLUE CHEESE, CRUMBLED |
| 4 OZ. | CREAM CHEESE |
| 1 TBSP. | SOFT BUTTER |
| 1 TBSP. | FINELY CHOPPED, GREEN ONION |
| 1½ TSP. | WORCESTERSHIRE SAUCE |
| 1 TBSP. | CREAM |
| 1/8 TSP. | SALT |
| 16 SLICES | RYE BREAD |
| 2 LBS. | COLD ROAST BEEF |
| | SALT |
| | PEPPER |

COMBINE FIRST 7 INGREDIENTS, BLEND UNTIL SMOOTH. COVER AND REFRIGERATE 4 HOURS, THEN BRING TO ROOM TEMPERATURE BEFORE USING. SPREAD 1 TBSP. CHEESE MIXTURE ON EACH SLICE OF BREAD, THEN TOP 8 SLICES WITH 1/4 LB. OF VERY THINLY SLICED ROAST BEEF. SPRINKLE WITH SALT AND PEPPER, COVER WITH TOP SLICE OF BREAD, AND CUT IN HALVES.

SERVES 8

REUBEN SANDWICHES

# SHRIMP PARTY SANDWICHES

3 OZ.      CREAM CHEESE
2 TBSP.  MAYONNAISE
1 TBSP.  CATSUP
1 TSP.    PREPARED MUSTARD
1/8 TSP.  GARLIC POWDER
1 CUP    SMALL COOKED SHRIMP
1/4 CUP  FINELY CHOPPED, CELERY
1 TSP.    FINELY CHOPPED, GREEN ONION
10 SLICES BUTTERED BREAD ,
         BROWN AND WHITE

    FOLD CREAM CHEESE,
MAYONNAISE, CATSUP, MUSTARD AND
GARLIC POWDER. STIR IN SHRIMP,
CELERY AND GREEN ONION. DIVIDE
FILLING EVENLY AMONG 5 BROWN
BREAD SLICES ; TOP EACH WITH A
WHITE BREAD SLICE. TRIM OFF THE
CRUSTS , AND CUT DIAGONALLY
INTO 4 TRIANGLES. THESE ARE
ALWAYS A FAVORITE AT A LADIES'
TEA OR LUNCHEON.

SERVES  8-10

# Reuben Sandwiches

2 CUPS SAUERKRAUT
1/4 GREEN PEPPER, DICED
2 GREEN ONIONS, DICED
2 TBSP. MAZOLA OIL
1/2 TSP. SALT
1/4 TSP. PEPPER
16 OZ. MOZZARELLA CHEESE, SLICED
16 SLICES CORNED BEEF
16 SLICES COLD ROAST TURKEY
16 SLICES RYE BREAD
1/2 LB. BUTTER

I USE MY OWN HOMEMADE SAUERKRAUT, BUT IF YOU MUST BUY IT, I'M SURE THAT YOU WILL FIND LIBBY'S WINE-CURED THE BEST. DRAIN THE SAUERKRAUT THROUGH A SIEVE, SQUEEZING OUT ALL THE JUICE, TURN INTO A BOWL, ADD GREEN PEPPER, ONION, MAZOLA OIL, SALT AND PEPPER. MIX WELL, REFRIGERATE FOR AN HOUR TO BLEND FLAVORS.

CONTINUED

LAY OUT THE 16 SLICES OF
BREAD, BUTTER SCANTILY, DIVIDE
SAUERKRAUT EVENLY AMONG
8 SLICES, TOP EACH WITH 2 SLICES
CORNED BEEF, A SLICE OF CHEESE,
2 SLICES TURKEY. TOP WITH A SLICE
OF BREAD, BUTTERED SIDE DOWN.
PRESS DOWN FIRMLY, BUTTER TOP SIDE,
PLACE IN FRYING PAN OVER MEDIUM
HEAT WITH BUTTERED SIDE DOWN.
NOW BUTTER THE LAST SIDE OF BREAD.
AN ELECTRIC FRYING PAN WORKS
PERFECTLY. SET ON 350° FRY TO A
GOLDEN BROWN, TURN AND REPEAT
ON OTHER SIDE. CUT IN HALF AND
SERVE WITH BOWLS OF YOUR
FAVORITE SOUP.

SERVES 8

# Egg Salad Sandwiches

| | |
|---|---|
| 8 | HARD-BOILED EGGS |
| 2 TBSP. | GREEN ONION |
| 1/4 CUP | GREEN PEPPER |
| 1/4 CUP | CELERY |
| 2 TBSP. | PIMENTO |
| 2 TBSP. | PARSLEY |
| 4 OZ. | CREAM CHEESE |
| 2 TBSP. | MAYONNAISE |
| 1 TSP. | CHILI SAUCE |
| 1 TSP. | SALT |
| 1/4 TSP. | PEPPER |

FINELY CHOP AND COMBINE FIRST 6 INGREDIENTS. BEAT THE REMAINING INGREDIENTS, ADD TO FIRST MIXTURE ; BLEND WELL. USE 3 TBSP. FILLING FOR EACH OF THE SANDWICHES. SHOULD MAKE ABOUT 8 SANDWICHES, WHICH CAN BE CUT IN THIRDS AND SERVED WITH BABY DILL PICKLES.

SERVES 8 to 10

# PICKLED EGGS

2½ CUPS VINEGAR
2 CUPS WATER
1½ TSP. COARSE PICKLING SALT
1½ TSP. MIXED PICKLING SPICE
1 SMALL BAY LEAF
12 FRESH EGGS
1 LARGE WHITE ONION

BOIL VINEGAR, WATER AND SALT FOR 5 MINUTES. TIE SPICE AND BAY LEAF IN A PIECE OF CHEESECLOTH. REMOVE BRINE FROM HEAT, ADD SPICE BAG AND LET COOL. PUT EGGS IN LARGE SAUCE PAN, COVER WITH COLD WATER, BRING TO A BOIL, COVER, THEN REMOVE FROM HEAT. LET SIT 20 MINUTES, DRAIN, COVER WITH COLD WATER FOR 5 MINUTES, THEN PEEL. SLICE ONION AND SEPARATE INTO RINGS. PLACE EGGS IN JAR, ALTERNATING WITH ONION RINGS, AND POUR COOLED BRINE OVER. COVER AND REFRIGERATE FOR 2 DAYS BEFORE USING.

MAKES 2 QTS.

# Cinnamon Loaf

1/4 CUP   BUTTER
1  CUP    SUGAR
2         EGGS
1  CUP    SOUR MILK *
1  TSP.   VANILLA
2  CUPS   FLOUR
1/2 TSP.  SODA
1  TSP.   BAKING POWDER
1/2 TSP.  SALT
2  TBSP.  SUGAR (MIX WITH CINNAMON)
1  TBSP.  CINNAMON

CREAM TOGETHER BUTTER AND SUGAR, ADD EGGS, MIX FOR 2 MINUTES AT MEDIUM SPEED. ADD MILK, VANILLA AND MIX. SIFT FLOUR, SODA, BAKING POWDER, AND SALT. ADD TO LIQUID AND MIX 3 MINUTES. GREASE AND LIGHTLY FLOUR A 9"x5" LOAF PAN. POUR IN 1/3 OF BATTER, TOP WITH 1 TBSP. SUGAR AND CINNAMON, REPEAT TWICE. MIX SLIGHTLY. BAKE AT 350° ABOUT 45 MINUTES. * TO SOUR MILK, USE 1 TBSP. VINEGAR WITH 1 CUP OF MILK.

MAKES 1 LOAF

# LEMON LOAF

½ CUP    BUTTER
1   CUP    SUGAR
2   TSP.    GRATED LEMON RIND
2           EGGS, BEATEN
½ CUP    MILK
1½ CUPS FLOUR
2   TSP.    BAKING POWDER
½ TSP.    SALT
2   TBSP. LEMON JUICE
1   TSP.    SUGAR

CREAM BUTTER, SUGAR, LEMON RIND, ADD EGGS AND MILK. SIFT FLOUR, BAKING POWDER AND SALT. MIX WELL, POUR INTO GREASED AND LIGHTLY FLOURED LOAF PAN, 9" x 5". BAKE AT 350° ABOUT 45 MINUTES, CHECK WITH A TOOTHPICK. MEANWHILE COMBINE LEMON JUICE AND SUGAR; ONCE COOKED POUR OVER TOP OF LOAF. COOL IN PAN BEFORE TURNING OUT ONTO RACK.

MAKES 1 LOAF

# KAHLUA CINNAMON BUNS

BUNS:
1 TSP.     SUGAR
¼ CUP      WARM WATER
1 PKG.     YEAST
⅓ CUP      SCALDING HOT MILK (COOLED)
¼ CUP      BUTTER
¼ CUP      SUGAR
½ TSP.     SALT
2½ CUPS    FLOUR
1 LARGE EGG

FOR BUNS DISSOLVE 1 TSP. SUGAR IN WATER. SPRINKLE YEAST OVER, LET STAND 10 MINUTES. STIR. COMBINE HOT MILK, BUTTER, SUGAR AND SALT IN MIXING BOWL. ADD 1 CUP FLOUR AND MIX WELL. FOLD IN BEATEN EGG, YEAST AND 1¼ CUPS FLOUR. TURN OUT ONTO FLOURED SURFACE AND KNEAD UNTIL SMOOTH. PLACE IN BOWL, GREASE WITH BUTTER, COVER WITH WAX PAPER AND A DAMP TOWEL. LET RISE ABOUT 1 HOUR IN WARM PLACE.

CONTINUED

FILLING:
1/4 CUP   SOFTENED BUTTER
1/3 CUP   SUGAR
2 TSP.   CINNAMON
1 TBSP.  KAHLUA
1/3 CUP   CHOPPED RAISINS

BEAT BUTTER, SUGAR AND CINNAMON TOGETHER UNTIL SMOOTH. MIX KAHLUA WITH RAISINS, THEN ADD AND BLEND.

SYRUP:
1/4 CUP   BUTTER
1/3 CUP   BROWN SUGAR
1 TBSP.  CORN SYRUP
1/4 CUP   KAHLUA

COMBINE ALL INGREDIENTS IN A SMALL SAUCEPAN. BRING TO A SIMMER THEN REMOVE FROM HEAT.

CONTINUED

63

PREPARE FILLING AND
SYRUP. ONCE DOUGH HAS RISEN
TO DOUBLE IN SIZE, PUNCH DOWN
AND LET REST 5 MINUTES. GREASE
A 9" TUBE PAN, THEN ROLL DOUGH
OUT ON A LIGHTLY FLOURED SURFACE
TO APPROXIMATELY 16"×12". SPREAD
ON FILLING, ROLL UP LIKE A JELLY
ROLL, SEAL EDGES BY PINCHING DOUGH
TOGETHER. CUT INTO 12 EVEN SLICES.
POUR ALL BUT 1/3 CUP OF SYRUP INTO
GREASED PAN. ARRANGE SLICES IN
PAN AND COVER WITH GREASED WAX
PAPER. LET RISE UNTIL ALMOST
DOUBLE IN SIZE, ABOUT 30 MINUTES.
BAKE IN PREHEATED 375° OVEN FOR
20 TO 25 MINUTES, UNTIL NICELY
BROWNED. AFTER THEY HAVE
COOKED, LET STAND IN PAN FOR
5 MINUTES THEN TURN UPSIDE DOWN
ON SERVING PLATE AND SPOON
REMAINING SYRUP OVER TOP. THESE
ARE REALLY DELICIOUS SERVED WARM.

MAKES 12 BUNS

64

# CARROT PINEAPPLE MUFFINS

1½ CUPS FLOUR
1 TSP. SALT
1 TSP. BAKING POWDER
1 TSP. SODA
1 TSP. CINNAMON
½ CUP BROWN SUGAR
2 TBSP. LIQUID HONEY
2 EGGS, BEATEN
2/3 CUP MAZOLA OIL
½ CUP CRUSHED PINEAPPLE
1 CUP SHREDDED CARROTS

MIX DRY INGREDIENTS, BLEND IN ALL OTHER INGREDIENTS UNTIL BATTER IS MOIST. LINE LARGE MUFFIN PANS WITH FOIL LINERS, FILL 2/3 FULL, BAKE AT 400° FOR 15 TO 20 MINUTES. SERVE WARM WITH BUTTER.

MAKES 12 MUFFINS.

# Carrot Cake

| | |
|---|---|
| 1¼ CUPS | MAZOLA OIL |
| 2 CUPS | SUGAR |
| 4 | EGGS |
| 3 CUPS | FLOUR |
| 2 TSP. | BAKING POWDER |
| 2 TSP. | BAKING SODA |
| 1 TSP. | SALT |
| 2 TSP. | CINNAMON |
| ½ TSP. | NUTMEG |
| ½ TSP. | CLOVES |
| ½ TSP. | ALLSPICE |
| ½ CUP | WALNUTS |
| 1 CUP | RAISINS |
| ½ CUP | CRUSHED PINEAPPLE |
| 3 CUPS | GRATED CARROTS |

COMBINE OIL AND SUGAR UNTIL SMOOTH. ADD EGGS 1 AT A TIME WITH MIXER AT MEDIUM SPEED. SIFT TOGETHER FLOUR, BAKING POWDER, SODA, SALT, AND SPICES. MIX WELL. ADD ALL OTHER INGREDIENTS, BLEND. BAKE IN A GREASED ANGEL FOOD PAN, 350° FOR 1 HOUR AND 20 MINUTES.

SERVES 18-20

# CRANBERRY BREAD

| | |
|---|---|
| 1 TSP. | SUGAR |
| ½ CUP | WARM WATER |
| 1 PKG. | YEAST |
| ½ CUP | MILK |
| ¼ CUP | BUTTER |
| 1 TSP. | SALT |
| ½ TSP. | NUTMEG |
| 3 TBSP. | SUGAR |
| 2 | LARGE EGGS |
| 1 TSP. | GRATED LEMON RIND |
| 4 CUPS | FLOUR |
| 1 | EGG WHITE, LIGHTLY BEATEN |

DISSOLVE SUGAR IN WARM WATER, SPRINKLE YEAST OVER AND LET STAND IN A WARM PLACE FOR 10 MINUTES. STIR. IN A SMALL SAUCEPAN, HEAT MILK AND BUTTER JUST UNTIL LUKEWARM. IN A LARGE MIXING BOWL PUT MILK, SALT, NUTMEG, 3 TBSP. SUGAR, EGGS, LEMON RIND, AND DISSOLVED YEAST. ADD 1 CUP FLOUR AND BEAT WITH MIXER UNTIL SMOOTH.

CONTINUED

WITH A WOODEN SPOON MIX IN ENOUGH OF REMAINING FLOUR TO MAKE A STIFF DOUGH. TURN OUT ON A FLOURED SURFACE AND KNEAD UNTIL SMOOTH AND ELASTIC. PLACE DOUGH IN A BOWL GREASED WITH BUTTER, TURN TO GREASE TOP, COVER WITH A DAMP TOWEL AND LET RISE IN A WARM PLACE UNTIL DOUBLE IN SIZE, ABOUT 1½ HOURS. PREPARE FILLING; PUNCH DOWN DOUGH, LET REST 5 MINUTES. CUT IN HALF ON A LIGHTLY FLOURED SURFACE, ROLL TO ABOUT 18" x 10", BRUSH WITH A BIT OF BEATEN EGG WHITE, THEN SPRINKLE WITH HALF OF CRANBERRY MIXTURE TO WITHIN 1" OF EDGES. ROLL UP LIKE A JELLY ROLL, SEAL ENDS AND LONG EDGE. PLACE SEAM SIDE DOWN ON GREASED, LIGHTLY FLOURED BAKING SHEET.

CONTINUED

REPEAT SAME PROCEDURE
WITH OTHER HALF OF DOUGH. BRUSH
WITH EGG WHITE. LET RISE ABOUT
45 MINUTES. BAKE IN PREHEATED
375° OVEN 40 TO 45 MINUTES.
SERVE WITH POULTRY, BAKED HAM
OR ROAST PORK.

FILLING:
1/4 CUP    SOFT BUTTER
1/2 CUP    SUGAR
1/4 CUP    FLOUR
1/2 CUP    CHOPPED WALNUTS
1  CUP     CHOPPED CRANBERRIES
1/2 TSP.   GRATED LEMON RIND

CREAM BUTTER AND SUGAR,
BLEND IN FLOUR, WALNUTS,
CRANBERRIES AND LEMON RIND.
CHILL UNTIL FIRM.

MAKES 2 LOAVES

# NOTES

PACIFIC COAST SALMON
PG. 95
BLUE DANUBE
FETTUCINE
PG. 110
MUSHROOM CHEESE
SALAD
PG. 84

# SOUPS AND SALADS

# CREAM OF ASPARAGUS

1 LB.      FRESH ASPARAGUS
½ CUP      BOILING WATER
2 CUPS     DICED POTATOES
1 TSP.     SALT
¼ TSP.     PEPPER
4 CUPS     CHICKEN STOCK
½ CUP      WHIPPING CREAM
¼ TSP.     SALT

WASH AND TRIM ASPARAGUS, PUT IN A LARGE SAUCEPAN. ADD WATER, COVER, COOK OVER MEDIUM HEAT UNTIL TENDER. LIFT THE ASPARAGUS FROM WATER, AND COOK POTATOES IN SAME WATER. WITHOUT DRAINING POUR INTO BLENDER, ADD ASPARAGUS, SALT, PEPPER, 1 CUP CHICKEN STOCK AND BLEND UNTIL SMOOTH. RETURN TO SAUCEPAN WITH REMAINING STOCK. BRING TO A BOIL, STIRRING, AND SIMMER. WHIP CREAM WITH ¼ TSP. SALT UNTIL STIFF, USE TO GARNISH WITH A FEW ASPARAGUS TIPS.

SERVES  6

# Manhatten Clam Chowder

3 SLICES  BACON, FINELY DICED
1 QT.        BOILING WATER
1½ TSP.    SALT
1 CUP      FINELY DICED CARROT
1 CUP      FINELY DICED CELERY
1 CUP      FINELY DICED ONION
2 CUPS    DICED POTATOES
2 CUPS    STEWED TOMATOES
10 OZ.      BABY CLAMS, JUICE
½ TSP.    THYME
¼ TSP.    PEPPER

IN A LARGE SOUP POT, LIGHTLY FRY BACON, ADD WATER, SALT, VEGETABLES AND TOMATOES. BRING TO A BOIL, SIMMER 20 TO 30 MINUTES. ADD CLAM JUICE, THYME AND PEPPER, SIMMER FOR ANOTHER 10 MINUTES. ADD CLAMS, HEAT THROUGH AND SERVE.

SERVES    4

75

# Egg Drop Soup

8 CUPS   BEEF STOCK
1 TBSP.   FINELY MINCED FRESH PARSLEY
½ TSP.   SALT
¼ TSP.   PEPPER

EGG DROPS:
2           EGGS
1 TBSP.   COLD WATER
½ TSP.   SALT
2/3 CUP   FLOUR

COMBINE BEEF STOCK, PARSLEY, SALT AND PEPPER; BRING TO A BOIL. BREAK EGGS INTO A BOWL, BEAT WITH A FORK, ADD WATER, SALT AND FLOUR TO MAKE A THICK PASTE. WHEN THE STOCK COMES TO A BOIL, DIP A SOUP SPOON INTO HOT STOCK, THEN INTO BATTER, GETTING ONLY ½ TSP. OF BATTER. PUT SPOON BACK INTO STOCK AND THE DUMPLING WILL SLIDE OFF. REPEAT UNTIL ALL BATTER IS USED. COOK 2 TO 3 MINUTES AND SERVE, AS THE DUMPLINGS WILL GET TOUGH IF COOKED TO LONG.

SERVES 4

# French Onion Soup

½ CUP    BUTTER
2  LARGE SPANISH ONIONS
½ TSP.   FRESHLY GROUND BLACK PEPPER
2 TBSP. PARMESAN CHEESE
1½ CUPS  DRY RED WINE
3  10 OZ. CANS BEEF BOUILLON
30 OZ.    WATER
1  LOAF  FRENCH BREAD
8  OZ.    GRUYERE CHEESE, SHREDDED
2 TBSP. PARMESAN CHEESE

        MELT BUTTER IN LARGE SOUP
POT, FRY THINLY SLICED ONIONS UNTIL
TRANSPARENT, ABOUT ½ HOUR. ADD
NEXT FIVE INGREDIENTS AND BRING TO
A BOIL, THEN SIMMER FOR 1 HOUR.
COVER AND LET SIT OVERNIGHT. TO SERVE;
HEAT SOUP, TOAST BREAD AND PLACE
A SLICE FOR EACH BOWL OF SOUP ON
TOP, WITH 1⅓ OZ. SHREDDED CHEESE
AND SPRINKLE WITH PARMESAN. TURN
OVEN TO BROIL, PLACE OVENPROOF BOWLS
ON MIDDLE RACK AND BROIL UNTIL
CHEESE IS GOLDEN BROWN. LET COOL
2 MINUTES BEFORE
SERVING.

SERVES  6

# SAUERKRAUT SOUP

4   SLICES BACON, FINELY CHOPPED
1   QT.    WATER
1          POTATO DICED
1          ONION, FINELY CHOPPED
1          CARROT, FINELY CHOPPED
2   CUPS   SAUERKRAUT WITH JUICE
1/2 TSP.   SALT
1/4 TSP.   PEPPER

    USING A LARGE SOUP POT, FRY
BACON, ADD WATER, POTATO, ONION,
AND CARROT. BRING TO A BOIL, THEN
SIMMER UNTIL VEGETABLES ARE
ALMOST TENDER. ADD SAUERKRAUT,
SALT AND PEPPER TO TASTE, SIMMER
AGAIN ABOUT 30 MINUTES. TASTE FOR
SEASONING AND SERVE. IF YOU FIND
THE SAUERKRAUT FLAVOR TOO STRONG,
ADD MORE WATER AND SIMMER FOR
ANOTHER 15 MINUTES.

SERVES  4

# Cabbage Soup

| | | |
|---|---|---|
| 2 | LBS. | SOUP BONES, WITH MEAT |
| 1 | TSP. | SALT |
| 1 | | BAY LEAF |
| ½ | TSP. | THYME |
| 1 | MEDIUM ONION, CHOPPED | |
| 3 | | CARROTS, CHOPPED |
| 2 | | POTATOES, DICED |
| ½ | CUP | DICED CELERY |
| ½ | CUP | SLICED MUSHROOMS |
| 3 | CUPS | CHOPPED CABBAGE |
| 1 | CLOVE | GARLIC, CRUSHED |
| 1 | TBSP. | LEMON JUICE |
| ½ | TSP. | SALT |
| ¼ | TSP. | PEPPER |

COVER BONES WITH COLD WATER, ADD SALT, BAY LEAF, AND THYME; BRING TO A BOIL. COVER AND SIMMER AT LEAST 3 HOURS. STRAIN, SKIM OFF FAT, RETURN TO SOUP POT. ADD THE ONION, CARROTS, POTATO, CELERY AND MUSHROOMS. COOK 30 MINUTES. ADD CABBAGE, COOK UNTIL TENDER, ABOUT 20 MINUTES. STIR IN GARLIC. ADD LEMON JUICE, SALT AND PEPPER TO TASTE.

SERVES 4-6

79

# Oriental Spinach Salad

2 TBSP.   SESAME SEEDS
½ CUP    OLIVE OIL
2 TBSP.   LEMON JUICE
1 TBSP.   SOY SAUCE
½ TSP.    SUGAR
¼ TSP.    SALT
⅛ TSP.    PEPPER
12 OZ.     SPINACH LEAVES
1 CUP     SLICED, MUSHROOMS

PUT SESAME SEEDS ON COOKIE SHEET AND TOAST IN OVEN 5 TO 8 MINUTES AT 350°, THEN PLACE IN BLENDER, ADD OIL, LEMON JUICE, SOY SAUCE, SUGAR. BLEND UNTIL SEEDS ARE GROUND AND SAUCE THICKENS. ADD SALT AND PEPPER TO TASTE, COVER AND REFRIGERATE. WASH AND DRY SPINACH LEAVES, BREAK INTO PIECES, SLICE MUSHROOMS, TOSS LIGHTLY TOGETHER. ADD THE DRESSING, TOSS TO BLEND AND SERVE.

SERVES 4

# Mizeria Of Cucumbers

3 MEDIUM CUCUMBERS
1 TSP.   SALT
½ CUP   FINELY CHOPPED GREEN ONIONS
1 DASH  PEPPER
3 TBSP. VINEGAR
¼ CUP   SOUR CREAM

WASH CUCUMBERS AND RUN A FORK LENGTHWISE TO CUT GROOVES. SLICE VERY THINLY, SPRINKLE WITH SALT, LET SIT 15 MINUTES. DRAIN AND PRESS OUT LIQUID. MIX WITH ONION, PEPPER AND VINEGAR. LET STAND IN REFRIGERATOR 15 MINUTES. MIX IN SOUR CREAM AND SERVE AS A SALAD.

SERVES 4

# Caesar Salad

½ HEAD ROMAINE LETTUCE
1½       ANCHOVY FILLETS
1 CLOVE GARLIC
¼ TSP.   DRY HOT MUSTARD
2½ DASHES WORCESTERSHIRE SAUCE
1 TBSP. DRY BREAD CRUMBS
1 TBSP. LEMON JUICE
1        EGG YOLK
1½ TBSP. PARMESAN CHEESE
¼ CUP    OLIVE OIL
¾ CUP    CROUTONS

WASH AND DRY LETTUCE LEAVES, LET CHILL. PUT ANCHOVIES AND GARLIC THROUGH PRESS INTO A LARGE SALAD BOWL. ADD MUSTARD, WORCESTERSHIRE SAUCE AND BREAD CRUMBS. MIX WELL, ADD LEMON JUICE, EGG YOLK AND 1 TBSP. PARMESAN CHEESE. DRIZZLE OIL IN VERY SLOWLY WHILE BEATING VIGOROUSLY UNTIL THICK AND CREAMY. BREAK LETTUCE INTO PIECES OVER DRESSING, SPRINKLE WITH ½ TBSP. PARMESAN, ADD CROUTONS AND TOSS.

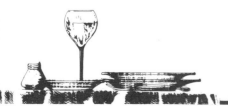

SERVES 4

# Red Cabbage Salad

3 CUPS    FINELY SHREDDED RED CABBAGE
1 CUP    CAULIFLOWER PIECES
2 TBSP.   SUGAR
2 TBSP.   VINEGAR
1/3 CUP    MIRACLE WHIP
1/4 TSP.   PREPARED MUSTARD
1/4 TSP.   TURMERIC

TOSS RED CABBAGE AND CAULIFLOWER TOGETHER. IN A SMALL BOWL MIX TOGETHER SUGAR, VINEGAR, MIRACLE WHIP, MUSTARD, AND TURMERIC. POUR DRESSING OVER CABBAGE, MIX WELL AND SET IN REFRIGERATOR FOR AT LEAST 2 HOURS TO CHILL BEFORE SERVING. THIS SALAD IS ESPECIALLY GOOD WITH A PORK ROAST.

SERVES 4

# Mushroom Cheese Salad

| | |
|---|---|
| 1 LB. | MUSHROOMS |
| 1 | RED ONION, THINLY SLICED |
| 1/3 CUP | OLIVE OIL |
| 1/4 CUP | RED WINE VINEGAR |
| 1/2 TSP. | SALT |
| 1/2 TSP. | SUGAR |
| 1/2 TSP. | DRIED LEAF CHERVIL |
| 1 PINCH | DRIED LEAF TARRAGON |
| 1 DASH | CAYENNE PEPPER |
| 1 CUP | OLD CHEDDAR, CUBED |
| 1/2 CUP | WATERCRESS LEAVES |
| 1 CUP | CROUTONS |

WIPE MUSHROOMS AND SLICE THINLY, SEPARATE ONION RINGS, TOSS INTO SALAD BOWL. MIX NEXT 7 INGREDIENTS IN A SMALL JAR, SHAKE WELL. POUR OVER MUSHROOMS AND ONIONS, TOSS AND CHILL 4 HOURS. ADD CHEESE CUBES, WATERCRESS AND CROUTONS AND TOSS JUST BEFORE SERVING.

SERVES 6

# Sauerkraut Salad

2 CUPS    SAUERKRAUT
2           GREEN ONIONS
½           GREEN PEPPER
2 TBSP. MAZOLA OIL
¼ TSP.    SALT
⅛ TSP.    PEPPER

       DRAIN SAUERKRAUT THROUGH A STRAINER, SQUEEZING OUT ALL OF THE JUICE. FINELY CHOP GREEN ONIONS AND GREEN PEPPER, ADD TO THE SAUERKRAUT, TOSS TO BLEND. ADD THE REST OF THE INGREDIENTS AND TOSS AGAIN. CHILL FOR 1 HOUR, TOSS BEFORE SERVING. IF USING HOMEMADE SAUERKRAUT SAVE THE JUICE IN A COVERED JAR IN REFRIGERATOR FOR SAUERKRAUT SOUP. THIS SALAD IS ESPECIALLY NICE SERVED WITH PORK DISHES.

SERVES 4

# Avocado Dressing

| | | |
|---|---|---|
| 2 | | AVOCADOS, PEELED AND PITTED |
| 1 | | ONION, CHOPPED |
| 1½ | CUPS | MAYONNAISE |
| ¼ | CUP | CIDER VINEGAR |
| 1 | | CLOVE GARLIC, CRUSHED |
| ½ | TSP. | SALT |
| ¼ | TSP. | PEPPER |
| 1 | DASH | WORCESTERSHIRE SAUCE |
| 4 | TBSP. | WHIPPING CREAM |

IN A BLENDER PURÉE AVOCADO, ONION AND MAYONNAISE. IN A MEDIUM BOWL MIX VINEGAR, GARLIC, SALT, PEPPER AND WORCESTERSHIRE, ADD AVOCADO MIXTURE. MIX WELL THEN BEAT IN CREAM UNTIL DESIRED CONSISTENCY IS REACHED. TASTE FOR SEASONING. COVER AND REFRIGERATE.

MAKES 2½ CUPS

# ANCHOVY CREAM DRESSING

| | |
|---|---|
| 1 CLOVE | GARLIC |
| 1 OZ. | ANCHOVY FILLETS |
| 1/4 CUP | GREEN ONION, FINELY CHOPPED |
| 1 1/2 TBSP. | LEMON JUICE |
| 1/4 CUP | TARRAGON VINEGAR |
| 1 PT. | WHIPPING CREAM |
| 1 CUP | MAYONNAISE |
| 1/4 CUP | MINCED FRESH PARSLEY |
| 1/4 TSP. | SALT |
| 1/8 TSP. | PEPPER |

PUT GARLIC AND ANCHOVIES THROUGH A GARLIC PRESS INTO A PINT JAR. ADD REMAINING INGREDIENTS, MIX THOROUGHLY AND CHILL. SERVE WITH A TOSSED GREEN SALAD.

MAKES 3 1/2 CUPS

# NOTES

# ENTRÉES

# Atlantic Lobster

| | | |
|---|---|---|
| 4 | | LIVE LOBSTERS |
| 6 QTS. | | WATER |
| 3 TBSP. | | COARSE PICKLING SALT |
| ½ | | LEMON SLICED |

LEMON BUTTER :

| | |
|---|---|
| ½ CUP | BUTTER, CLARIFIED |
| 2 TBSP. | LEMON JUICE |
| 1 DASH | GARLIC POWDER |

BUY 1½ LB. LOBSTERS FOR BEST FLAVOR AND TENDER MEAT. TO CHECK IF LOBSTER IS ALIVE, HOLD TAIL OUT STRAIGHT ; IT SHOULD SPRING BACK. TO COOK USE A LARGE POT, BRING WATER, SALT AND LEMON TO A BOIL. ADD LOBSTER HEAD FIRST. COVER POT, RETURN TO A BOIL, REDUCE HEAT AND COOK 20 MINUTES PER POUND. REMOVE LOBSTER FROM WATER, BREAK CLAWS WITH CLEAVER, CUT UNDERSIDE OF TAIL WITH SCISSORS. SERVE WITH LEMON BUTTER FOR DIPPING.

SERVES 4

# Whitefish Almondine

| 2 LBS. | WHITEFISH FILLETS |
|---|---|
| 1 TSP. | SALT |
| 1/8 TSP. | PEPPER |
| 1/2 CUP | MELTED BUTTER |
| 10 OZ. | CONDENSED CREAM OF MUSHROOM SOUP |
| 1/3 CUP | DRY WHITE WINE |
| 1/2 CUP | SLIVERED ALMONDS |
| 1 TBSP. | LEMON JUICE |

SPRINKLE FISH WITH SALT AND PEPPER, PLACE IN A SHALLOW BAKING PAN. DRIZZLE WITH 1/4 CUP MELTED BUTTER. COMBINE SOUP AND WINE IN SAUCEPAN OVER MEDIUM HEAT, BLEND UNTIL SMOOTH. POUR OVER FISH. BAKE UNCOVERED AT 350°, FOR 30 TO 40 MINUTES UNTIL FISH WILL FLAKE WITH A FORK. SAUTÉ ALMONDS IN 1/4 CUP BUTTER ADD LEMON JUICE, STIR AND POUR OVER FISH, SERVE HOT.

SERVES 4

# SOLE IN WINE SAUCE

| | |
|---|---|
| 8 | FILLETS OF SOLE |
| 8 | LARGE SHRIMP, CLEANED |
| ½ CUP | BUTTER |
| ¼ CUP | FINELY CHOPPED ONION |
| ⅔ CUP | DRY WHITE WINE |
| ¼ CUP | BRANDY |
| 1 CUP | SLICED MUSHROOM CAPS |
| 4 TSP. | MINCED PARSLEY |
| 1 TBSP. | FLOUR |
| 1 TBSP. | BUTTER MELTED |
| 4 | EGG YOLKS |
| 4 TSP. | WHIPPING CREAM |
| 1 TSP. | FISH AROMAT |
| ½ TSP. | SALT |

CONTINUED

92

PLACE 1 SHRIMP ON END OF EACH FILLET AND ROLL UP. MELT ½ CUP BUTTER IN FLAMEPROOF BAKING DISH; LIGHTLY COOK ONION. PLACE ROLLED FILLETS IN PAN, POUR WINE AND BRANDY OVER TOP. SPRINKLE WITH MUSHROOMS AND PARSLEY. COVER PAN WITH BUTTERED WAX PAPER. BAKE AT 350° FOR 20 MINUTES. REMOVE FILLETS. BLEND FLOUR AND MELTED BUTTER TO A SMOOTH PASTE, ADD TO SAUCE, STIRRING OVER LOW HEAT UNTIL THICKENED. WHISK EGG YOLKS WITH CREAM, ADD FISH AROMAT AND SALT. STIR INTO SAUCE. RETURN FILLETS TO BAKING PAN, POUR SAUCE OVER. SET OVEN TO BROIL, SET FILLETS ON THE MIDDLE RACK AND BROIL UNTIL GOLDEN BROWN. SERVE THE FILLETS WITH SAUCE ON A BED OF STEAMED RICE.

SERVES 4

# Oriental Steamed Trout

| | |
|---|---|
| 2 LB. | TROUT |
| 1 TSP. | GRATED FRESH GINGER |
| 2 TBSP. | SHERRY |
| 1/2 TSP. | SALT |
| 4 | GREEN ONIONS, CUT 1 1/2" LONG |
| 2 TBSP. | SESAME SEED OIL, VERY HOT |
| 2 TBSP. | SOY SAUCE |
| 2 TSP. | VINEGAR |
| 1/4 TSP. | GRATED FRESH GINGER |

WASH AND DRY TROUT, THEN RUB INSIDE WITH MIXTURE OF GINGER, SHERRY AND SALT. SLASH FISH 4 OR 5 TIMES ON EACH SIDE, 1/4" DEEP. STEAM ABOUT 15 MINUTES UNTIL TROUT IS FLAKY. TO MAKE SAUCE, COMBINE SOY SAUCE, VINEGAR AND GINGER IN SMALL PAN; WARM OVER LOW HEAT. PLACE TROUT ON SERVING DISH TOP WITH ONIONS THEN POUR SMOKING HOT OIL OVER. SERVE WITH LEMON WEDGES AND PARSLEY SPRIGS. USE BUTTER WARMERS FOR SAUCE TO KEEP IT HOT.

SERVES 2-4

# Pacific Coast Salmon

| | | |
|---|---|---|
| 2 | LB. | SALMON |
| 1/2 | TSP. | SALT |
| 1/4 | TSP. | PEPPER |
| 2 | TBSP. | BUTTER |
| 1 | LB. | MUSHROOMS, SLICED |
| 2 | TBSP. | LEMON JUICE |
| 1/8 | TSP. | CAYENNE PEPPER |
| 1 | TBSP. | MINCED PARSLEY |
| 1 | LB. | MEDIUM, COOKED SHRIMP |
| 2 | TBSP. | OLIVE OIL |
| 1 | TBSP. | BUTTER |

CLEAN, WASH AND DRY SALMON, LEAVE THE HEAD ON FOR FLAVOR. SALT AND PEPPER THE INSIDE. MELT BUTTER IN SAUCEPAN, ADD MUSHROOMS AND FRY GENTLY. ADD NEXT 4 INGREDIENTS, LET IT COOK GENTLY A FEW MINUTES. PLACE FISH ON A RACK, STUFF WITH HALF THE FILLING, CUT 1/2" SLASHES 1" APART AND BRUSH FISH WITH OIL AND BUTTER. BAKE ABOUT 20 MINUTES AT 375°. ARRANGE HEATED REMAINING STUFFING ALONG CUT SIDE. DECORATE WITH LEMON TWISTS AND PARSLEY SPRIGS.

SERVES 4

# Flambéed Shrimp

| 1½ LBS. | JUMBO SHRIMP |
| ½ TSP. | SALT |
| ¼ TSP. | PEPPER |
| 4 TBSP. | BUTTER |
| 1 TBSP. | FINELY CHOPPED GREEN ONION |
| 2 TBSP. | LEMON JUICE |
| ¼ CUP | COGNAC |

PEEL AND DEVEIN SHRIMP, SPRINKLE WITH SALT AND PEPPER. HEAT BUTTER IN A HEAVY SKILLET AND ADD THE SHRIMP. WHILE COOKING SHAKE SKILLET AND STIR CONSTANTLY. ADD GREEN ONIONS, SPRINKLE WITH LEMON JUICE, STIR AND ADD COGNAC. CONTINUE STIRRING UNTIL THE FLAME HAS EXTINGUISHED. SERVE WITH MUSHROOM RICE.

NOTE:    SINCE COOKING TIME FOR THE SHRIMP IS ONLY ABOUT 3 MINUTES WAIT UNTIL RICE IS READY AS THE SHRIMP MUST BE SERVED HOT.

SERVES 4

# Mushroom Rice

| | |
|---|---|
| ¼ LB. | MUSHROOMS |
| 1 TBSP. | BUTTER |
| ¼ CUP | FINELY CHOPPED ONION |
| ½ | BAY LEAF |
| 1 CUP | RAW RICE |
| 1½ CUPS | CHICKEN BROTH |

WIPE MUSHROOMS, TRIM ENDS. CUT CAPS AND STEMS INTO ½" CUBES. HEAT BUTTER IN SAUCEPAN, ADD ONION, MUSHROOMS, BAY LEAF AND RICE. STIR TO COAT RICE IN BUTTER. ADD CHICKEN BROTH AND BRING TO A BOIL. COVER AND SIMMER FOR 20 MINUTES. DISCARD BAY LEAF AND SERVE.

SERVES 4

# Oriental Cornish Hens

6 OZ. PKG. LONG-GRAIN AND WILD RICE
1/2 CUP      DICED CELERY
1/2 CUP      CHOPPED MUSHROOMS
2/3 CUP      SLICED WATER CHESTNUTS
4  TBSP.  BUTTER
1  TBSP.  SOY SAUCE
4 - 1 LB.  CORNISH HENS

COOK RICE FOLLOWING PACKAGE
DIRECTIONS, COOL, ADD NEXT 5 INGREDIENTS.
TOSS LIGHTLY TO MIX. WASH AND DRY
HENS, SALT INSIDE, THEN STUFF AND
TRUSS. ROAST AT 375°, COVERED
LOOSELY WITH ALUMINUM FOIL FOR
FIRST 30 MINUTES. UNCOVER AND
CONTINUE COOKING FOR ANOTHER
60 MINUTES BASTING WITH BUTTER 2 OR 3
TIMES. MAY BE SERVED WHOLE OR HALVED
WITH AN ELECTRIC KNIFE AND PUT CUT
SIDES DOWN ON INDIVIDUAL PLATES.

SERVES 4-6

# Curried Chicken Wings

| 18 | CHICKEN WINGS |
|---|---|
| 1 QT. | COLD WATER |
| 1 TSP. | SALT |
| 2 CUPS | BROTH, (SEE BELOW) |
| 1 LARGE | ONION, FINELY CHOPPED |
| 1 TBSP. | MAZOLA OIL |
| 2 TBSP. | FLOUR |
| 1 TBSP. | CURRY POWDER |
| 1 TBSP. | CHICKEN SOUP BASE |

PUT CHICKEN WINGS IN A POT WITH COLD WATER AND SALT. BRING TO A BOIL, SKIM, COVER AND SIMMER 45 MINUTES. REMOVE CHICKEN FROM STOCK, SET BOTH ASIDE. IN AN ELECTRIC FRYING PAN, FRY ONION IN OIL UNTIL SOFT. STIR IN FLOUR, CURRY POWDER AND SOUP BASE. THEN ADD STOCK SLOWLY, STIRRING UNTIL SMOOTH. TASTE FOR SEASONING; A BIT MORE SALT MAY BE NEEDED. ADD WINGS, MIX TO COAT WITH SAUCE. COVER AND SIMMER 1/2 HOUR. SERVE WITH STEAMED RICE.

SERVES 4-6

# POLYNESIAN CHICKEN

| 4 | | HALF CHICKEN BREASTS |
|---|---|---|
| 2 | TBSP. | BUTTER |
| 1/4 | TSP. | SALT |
| 1/8 | TSP. | PEPPER |
| 1 | | BANANA |
| 2 | | EGGS |
| 1/4 | CUP | MILK |
| 1/2 | CUP | FLOUR |
| 2 | CUPS | CORNFLAKE CRUMBS |

BONE CHICKEN BREASTS AND FLATTEN EACH WITH A CLEAVER. SPREAD EACH BREAST WITH BUTTER, SEASON WITH SALT AND PEPPER. PEEL BANANA, CUT IN 4 PIECES, PLACE 1 PIECE ON EACH BREAST, ROLL UP AND SECURE WITH A TOOTHPICK. BEAT EGGS; ADD MILK. ROLL CHICKEN IN FLOUR, DIP INTO EGG MIXTURE, AGAIN IN FLOUR, ONCE MORE IN EGG, THEN IN CORNFLAKE CRUMBS. FRY IN OIL OVER MEDIUM HEAT UNTIL GOLDEN BROWN. REMOVE PICKS AND PLACE CHICKEN IN A SMALL CASSEROLE DISH.

CONTINUED

## POLYNESIAN SAUCE:

| 16 OZ. | CAN PINEAPPLE CHUNKS |
|--------|---------------------|
| 2 TBSP. | CORNSTARCH |
| 1/4 CUP | BROWN SUGAR |
| 1/4 CUP | VINEGAR |
| 2 TBSP. | SOY SAUCE |
| 1 | GREEN PEPPER, CHOPPED |

DRAIN PINEAPPLE, ADD WATER TO JUICE TO MAKE 1 CUP. PLACE LIQUID IN SAUCEPAN, ADD CORNSTARCH, SUGAR, VINEGAR, AND SOY SAUCE. HEAT AND STIR UNTIL THICK AND CLEAR. ADD PINEAPPLE CHUNKS AND GREEN PEPPER; POUR OVER CHICKEN. PLACE IN PREHEATED 350° OVEN FOR 30 MINUTES.

SERVES 4

# BEEF WELLINGTON

| 2 LB.    | BEEF TENDERLOIN, TRIMMED  |
|----------|---------------------------|
| ¼ LB.    | FRESH MUSHROOMS, MINCED   |
| 1        | ONION, FINELY CHOPPED     |
| 1 TBSP.  | MELTED BUTTER             |
| 4 OZ.    | HERBED LIVERWURST         |
| 3 CUPS   | FLOUR                     |
| 1 TSP.   | SALT                      |
| 3 TBSP.  | MINCED PARSLEY            |
| ⅔ CUP    | SHORTENING                |
| ½ CUP    | COLD WATER                |
| 1        | EGG, LIGHTLY BEATEN       |

ONE DAY AHEAD, ROAST MEAT IN SHALLOW PAN AT 325° FOR 1 HOUR. LET COOL, WRAP AND REFRIGERATE. NEXT DAY, SAUTÉ MUSHROOMS AND ONION IN BUTTER UNTIL ONION IS SOFT AND TRANSPARENT. REMOVE FROM HEAT, MIX IN LIVERWURST, AND CHILL IN REFRIGERATOR.

CONTINUED

TO MAKE PASTRY; MIX FLOUR, SALT AND PARSLEY, CUT IN SHORTENING WITH PASTRY CUTTER. ADD COLD WATER SLOWLY, TOSSING MIXTURE WITH A FORK; ADD A BIT MORE WATER IF NECESSARY. SHAPE DOUGH INTO A BALL, ROLL OUT UNTIL ½" THICK. PAT LIVERWURST MIXTURE ON TOP AND SIDES OF COLD MEAT. PLACE MEAT, COATED SIDE DOWN, ON PASTRY. FOLD PASTRY UP TO MEET ALONG CENTER, FOLD UP ENDS, TRIM OFF EXTRA PASTRY, MOISTEN EDGES AND PRESS FIRMLY TO SEAL WELL. PLACE ROAST, SEALED EDGES DOWN, IN A GREASED PAN; BRUSH WITH BEATEN EGG. PRICK WITH A FORK TO ALLOW STEAM TO ESCAPE. BAKE IN PREHEATED OVEN AT 375° FOR 1 HOUR, UNTIL CRUST IS GOLDEN BROWN. LET STAND 15 MINUTES BEFORE SERVING, SLICE CAREFULLY.

SERVES 6-8

# PORK STROGANOFF

| | |
|---|---|
| 1½ LBS. | PORK TENDERLOIN |
| ¼ CUP | BUTTER |
| 1 | ONION, CHOPPED |
| ½ CUP | MADEIRA WINE |
| 10 OZ. | CAN BEEF BOUILLON (RESERVE ¼ CUP) |
| 1 LB. | FRESH MUSHROOMS, SLICED |
| ½ TSP. | SALT |
| ¼ TSP. | PEPPER |
| 1 TSP. | SUMMER SAVORY |
| 1 TBSP. | FLOUR |
| ¾ CUP | SOUR CREAM |

CUT MEAT IN ½" SLICES. MELT BUTTER IN A 2-QUART CASSEROLE, ADD ONION AND PORK. COOK AND STIR UNTIL PORK TURNS COLOR, ABOUT 5 MINUTES. ADD MADEIRA AND ALLOW TO BOIL, STIRRING CONSTANTLY. ADD BOUILLON AND MUSHROOMS, SALT, PEPPER AND SAVORY. COOK 30 MINUTES. MIX FLOUR AND EXTRA BROTH, STIR INTO SAUCE AND COOK 5 MINUTES. BLEND IN SOUR CREAM AND SERVE.

SERVES 4

# Black Peppercorn Steak

| | |
|---|---|
| 2 LB. | SIRLOIN, CUT IN 4 SERVINGS |
| ½ TSP. | SALT |
| 2 TBSP. | BLACK PEPPERCORNS, GROUND |
| 1 TBSP. | OLIVE OIL |
| 3 TBSP. | BUTTER |
| 1 CLOVE | GARLIC |
| 2 TBSP. | COGNAC |
| ½ CUP | WHIPPING CREAM |

TRIM FAT FROM STEAK, SPRINKLE WITH SALT AND PEPPERCORNS, LET SIT 2 HOURS. ADD OIL, BUTTER AND GARLIC CLOVE SPLIT IN HALF TO HOT FRYING PAN OVER HIGH HEAT. FRY STEAK 5 MINUTES THEN TURN AND FRY UNTIL THE BLOOD BREAKS THROUGH TOP. TURN OFF HEAT, ADD COGNAC AND FLAME. REMOVE STEAK TO HOT SERVING PLATES, DISCARD GARLIC. ADD CREAM, STIR SAUCE AND POUR OVER STEAKS. SERVE IMMEDIATELY.

SERVES 4

# NOTES

# INTERNATIONAL CLASSICS

# Blue Danube Fettucine

| | | |
|---|---|---|
| 1 | CUP | BLUE CHEESE, CRUMBLED |
| 1/4 | CUP | BUTTER |
| 1 | CUP | WHIPPING CREAM |
| 1/4 | CUP | MINCED, FRESH PARSLEY |
| 1/2 | TSP. | SALT |
| 1/4 | TSP. | PEPPER |
| 1/4 | TSP. | CAYENNE PEPPER |
| 8 | OZ. | FRESH FETTUCINE NOODLES |

IN A SAUCEPAN BLEND 3/4 CUP CHEESE, BUTTER, CREAM, PARSLEY, SALT, PEPPER AND CAYENNE. STIR OVER LOW HEAT UNTIL SMOOTH. IN A LARGE POT BOIL 2 QUARTS OF WATER, ADD NOODLES, STIR TO SEPARATE. BRING BACK TO A BOIL, COOK 3 MINUTES; DRAIN, ADD TO HEATED SAUCE AND BLEND. TURN ONTO SERVING PLATTER, SPRINKLE WITH REMAINING CHEESE AND SERVE.

SERVES 4-6

# Italian Tomato Sauce

4 CUPS STEWED TOMATOES
1/4 CUP OLIVE OIL
1 CUP FINELY CHOPPED ONION
1 CLOVE GARLIC, CRUSHED
6 OZ. TOMATO PASTE
1 TBSP. CHOPPED PARSLEY
1 TBSP. SALT
2 TSP. SUGAR
1 TSP. OREGANO
1 TSP. BASIL
1/4 TSP. CAYENNE PEPPER
1/4 TSP. PEPPER
1 DASH TABASCO
1/4 TSP. WORCESTERSHIRE SAUCE
2 TBSP. LEMON JUICE
1 1/2 CUPS WATER

ADD ALL INGREDIENTS IN A LARGE POT, MIX WELL. BRING TO A BOIL, STIRRING CONSTANTLY, REDUCE HEAT AND SIMMER, COVERED FOR 1 HOUR, STIRRING AT LEAST OCCASIONALLY.

MAKES 7 CUPS

# LASAGNE

| | | |
|---|---|---|
| 1½ LBS. | | LEAN GROUND BEEF |
| 1 | CUP | FINELY CHOPPED ONION |
| ½ | | GREEN PEPPER, DICED |
| 2 CLOVES GARLIC, CRUSHED | | |
| 2 | TBSP. | SUGAR |
| 1 | TBSP. | SALT |
| 1½ | TSP. | DRIED BASIL LEAVES |
| 1 | TSP. | OREGANO |
| ¼ | TSP. | PEPPER |
| ½ | CUP | MINCED PARSLEY |
| 4 | CUPS | STEWED TOMATOES   PG. 116 |
| 5½ | OZ. | TOMATO PASTE |
| ½ | TSP. | CRUSHED RED PEPPERS |
| 6 | CUPS | CREAMY COTTAGE CHEESE |
| 4 | | EGGS, WELL BEATEN |
| ¼ | CUP | MINCED PARSLEY |
| 2 | TSP. | SALT |
| 1 | TSP. | PEPPER |
| 1 | CUP | PARMESAN CHEESE |
| 12 | | WIDE LASAGNE NOODLES |
| ½ | TSP. | SALT |
| ½ | TSP. | OLIVE OIL |
| 2 | CUPS | ITALIAN TOMATO SAUCE PG. 111 |
| 2 | LBS. | MOZZARELLA, SLICED |

CONTINUED

112

BROWN GROUND BEEF IN A
LARGE FRYING PAN. ADD NEXT 12
INGREDIENTS, MIX WELL. BRING TO A
BOIL, THEN SIMMER 1 HOUR, STIRRING
OCCASIONALLY. MAKE CHEESE FILLING
BY COMBINING NEXT 6 INGREDIENTS.
COOK LASAGNE NOODLES IN A LARGE
POT USING 4 QUARTS WATER, SALT AND
OLIVE OIL, OVER HIGH HEAT UNTIL
TENDER. DRAIN, RINSE IN COLD WATER.
OIL A 13" x 9" BAKING PAN. SPREAD
1 CUP ITALIAN TOMATO SAUCE ON
BOTTOM, THEN 1 LAYER OF NOODLES,
HALF THE COTTAGE CHEESE MIXTURE
SPREAD EVENLY, HALF THE MOZZARELLA,
THEN HALF THE MEAT SAUCE SPREAD
EVENLY. REPEAT LAYERS, TOP WITH
LASAGNA NOODLES, THEN SPREAD
REST OF TOMATO SAUCE OVER TOP.
BAKE AT 375° FOR 45 MINUTES. REMOVE
FROM OVEN AND LET SET 20 MINUTES
BEFORE SERVING.

SERVES 8-12

# Italian Antipasto

| | | |
|---|---|---|
| 1 | CUP | OLIVE OIL |
| 1 | CUP | CHOPPED ONION |
| 1 | CUP | DICED CARROTS |
| 1 | CUP | DICED CELERY |
| 1 | CUP | DICED GREEN PEPPER |
| 1 | CUP | BUTTON MUSHROOMS |
| 1 | CUP | SMALL CAULIFLOWER FLORETS |
| 4 | TBSP. | LEMON JUICE |
| 1 | CUP | WINE VINEGAR |
| 32 | OZ. | CATSUP |
| 32 | OZ. | CHILI SAUCE |
| 1 | CUP | STUFFED OLIVES |
| 1 | CUP | PITTED BLACK OLIVES |
| 1 | CUP | SWEET RED PIMENTO |
| 1 | CUP | PEARL ONIONS |
| 3 | CLOVES | GARLIC |
| 1 | TSP. | WHITE PEPPER |
| 1 | TSP. | OREGANO |
| 3 | | BAY LEAVES |
| ½ | TSP. | POWDERED MARJORAM |
| 6 | | CLOVES |
| ½ | CUP | CHOPPED PARSLEY |
| 13 | OZ. | CHUNK TUNA |

CONTINUED

114

HEAT OIL IN LARGE SAUCEPAN, SAUTÉ ONION, ADD CARROTS, CELERY, GREEN PEPPER, MUSHROOMS AND CAULIFLOWER, STIRRING JUST TO STEAM. ADD LEMON JUICE AND VINEGAR. BLEND IN CATSUP AND CHILI SAUCE. STIR WELL. BRING TO A BOIL, THEN ALLOW TO SIMMER 20 MINUTES. WATCH IT DOESN'T STICK TO BOTTOM. ADD REMAINING INGREDIENTS EXCEPT FOR TUNA, BRING TO A BOIL, COOK 5 MINUTES STIRRING CONSTANTLY. REMOVE FROM HEAT, ADD TUNA, MIX WELL. PUT IN PINT JARS AND A DEEP WATER BATH FOR 35 MINUTES.

NOTE : ANTIPASTO IS AN HORS D'OEUVRE TO BE SERVED ON YOUR FAVORITE CRACKERS, SO KEEP IN MIND WHEN CUTTING UP INGREDIENTS AS YOU DON'T WANT YOUR PIECES TOO LARGE.

MAKES 14 PINTS

# STEWED TOMATOES

50 LBS. TOMATOES
6        STALKS CELERY
6        LARGE ONIONS
3        GREEN PEPPERS
1/4 CUP  PEPPERCORNS
20       BAY LEAVES
20 TSP.  PICKLING SALT

WASH TOMATOES, DIP INTO BOILING WATER 2 MINUTES, THEN INTO COLD WATER. REMOVE SKINS AND CORE, CUT INTO QUARTERS. FOR VEGETABLE MIXTURE CUT ABOUT 10 LBS. TOMATOES INTO LARGE POT. COOK ON MEDIUM HEAT. ADD DICED VEGETABLES ONCE POT STARTS TO BOIL. BRING TO A BOIL AND SIMMER 20 MINUTES. PACK REMAINING TOMATOES INTO HOT STERILIZED QUART JARS TO 3/4 FULL. REMOVE ALL AIR. TOP WITH VEGETABLE MIXTURE, ADD 1 TSP. PICKLING SALT, 5 PEPPERCORNS AND 1 BAY LEAF. SEAL AND PROCESS 45 MINUTES IN A PRESSURE CANNER.

MAKES 20 QTS.

# STUFFED GREEN PEPPERS

| 4 |  | GREEN PEPPERS |
|---|---|---|
| 1 | LB. | LEAN GROUND BEEF |
| 1 | CUP | COOKED RICE |
| 1 |  | ONION, FINELY CHOPPED |
| 2 |  | EGGS, BEATEN |
| 1/2 | TSP. | PAPRIKA |
| 1/2 | TSP. | SALT |
| 1/8 | TSP. | PEPPER |
| 2 | CUPS | TOMATO JUICE |
| 5 1/2 | OZ. | CAN TOMATO PASTE |
| 2 | TBSP. | BROWN SUGAR |
|  |  | SALT TO TASTE |
|  |  | PEPPER TO TASTE |

CUT TOPS OFF GREEN PEPPERS, CORE AND RINSE. MIX NEXT 7 INGREDIENTS AND STUFF INTO PEPPER SHELLS. IN A LARGE PAN ADD REST OF INGREDIENTS AND BRING TO A BOIL. SET PEPPERS UPRIGHT IN SAUCE, COVER, REDUCE HEAT AND SIMMER 45 MINUTES UNTIL TENDER. REMOVE PEPPERS TO SERVING DISH, SPOON SAUCE OVER PEPPERS AND SERVE.

SERVES 4

# Summer Beet Borsch

| | | |
|---|---|---|
| 2 | LBS. | PORK RIBLETS |
| 8 | | BEETS WITH TOPS |
| 1 | | ONION, CHOPPED |
| 1 | | POTATO, DICED |
| 2 | | CARROTS, DICED |
| 1 | CUP | SHELLED FRESH PEAS |
| 1 | CUP | DICED GREEN BEANS |
| 1 | STALK | CELERY DICED |
| 1 | CUP | SHREDDED CABBAGE |
| 1 | TBSP. | MINCED PARSLEY |
| 1 | TSP. | SALT |
| ½ | TSP. | PEPPER |

WASH BONES IN COLD WATER, PUT IN A LARGE SOUP POT, COVER WITH COLD WATER AND BRING TO A BOIL. SKIM OFF ANY FOAM, COVER AND SIMMER 4 HOURS. PEEL BEETS, THEN RINSE QUICKLY UNDER RUNNING WATER TO PREVENT BLEEDING, AS YOU WANT YOUR SOUP TO HAVE LOTS OF COLOR.

CONTINUED

SLICE BEETS IN NARROW STRIPS, SET ASIDE. PREPARE THE REST OF YOUR VEGETABLES. WHEN STOCK IS READY, ADD VEGETABLES, SALT AND PEPPER. BRING TO A BOIL, SIMMER 20 MINUTES, THEN ADD BEETS. SIMMER ANOTHER 15 MINUTES UNTIL BEETS ARE TENDER. TASTE FOR SEASONING; ADD SALT AND PEPPER TO YOUR LIKING. SERVE WITH A PITCHER OF HEAVY CREAM ON THE TABLE SO EVERYONE CAN ADD AS THEY WISH.

NOTE: LEFTOVER BORSCH SHOULD BE REFRIGERATED UNTIL LATER USE.

MAKES 2 QTS.

# STUDENETZ

| | | |
|---|---|---|
| 2 | | PIG'S FEET, SPLIT LENGTHWAYS |
| 2 | TSP. | SALT |
| 1 | | CARROT, CHOPPED |
| 1 | STALK | CELERY, WITH LEAVES |
| 1 | | ONION |
| 1 | CLOVE | GARLIC |
| 5 | | PEPPERCORNS |
| 1/2 | | BAY LEAF |
| 1 | TBSP. | VINEGAR |
| 1/2 | TBSP. | GELATIN |
| 1/4 | CUP | COLD WATER |

WASH AND SCRAPE THE FEET VERY THOROUGHLY, WIPE DRY, THEN PLACE UNDER THE BROILER UNTIL A DELICATE GOLDEN COLOR ON BOTH SIDES. PLACE FEET IN A LARGE POT, COVER WITH COLD WATER, ADD SALT, BRING TO A BOIL. SKIM, COVER AND SIMMER SLOWLY FOR 3 HOURS. DO NOT ALLOW TO BOIL.

CONTINUED

CUT ONION IN HALF AND BROWN IN UNGREASED PAN, THEN ADD TO PIG'S FEET WITH OTHER INGREDIENTS EXCEPT VINEGAR, GELATIN AND WATER. CONTINUE TO SIMMER ABOUT 2 HOURS, UNTIL MEAT COMES OFF THE BONES EASILY. STRAIN BROTH INTO A CLEAN POT, ADD VINEGAR AND SALT TO TASTE. REMOVE MEAT FROM BONES, CUT INTO SMALL PIECES, ADD A FEW SLIVERS OF COOKED CARROT, ARRANGE IN AN OBLONG GLASS PAN. MIX GELATIN IN COLD WATER, THEN ADD TO HOT BROTH. POUR BROTH OVER MEAT AND LET SET UNTIL FIRM. SKIM OFF ANY FAT WHILE STILL WARM. REFRIGERATE AND SERVE CHILLED, AS A SIDE DISH.

SERVES 10-12

# Kutya

½ CUP    HIGH GRADE WHITE WHEAT
              WATER TO COVER
¼ TSP.    SALT
½ CUP    LIQUID HONEY
1 CUP    WATER
¼ CUP    POPPY SEEDS
1 OZ.    SHAVED ALMONDS

      WASH WHEAT THOROUGHLY,
COVER WITH WARM WATER AND SOAK
OVERNIGHT. COOK IN SOAKING WATER,
BRING TO A BOIL, COVER AND
SIMMER FOR 2 TO 3 HOURS. STIR A
FEW TIMES WHILE COOKING. SALT
LIGHTLY BEFORE TOTALLY COOKED;
SHOULD BE THICK AND TENDER. MIX
HONEY AND WATER, BRING TO A BOIL
AND COOL. COMBINE SYRUP AND
WHEAT TO A MEDIUM THIN MIXTURE.
STIR IN POPPY SEEDS, TOP WITH ALMONDS.
THIS DISH IS SERVED WARM OR
CHILLED AT THE BEGINNING OF A
UKRAINIAN DINNER.

SERVES 6-8

# Caraway Pork Roast

4 LB.     PORK LOIN
2 TBSP.  FLOUR
1 TSP.    SALT
1/2 TSP. SUGAR
1 TSP.    DRY MUSTARD
1/8 TSP. PEPPER
1            ONION CHOPPED
2 TSP.    CARAWAY SEED
1 CUP     WATER

REMOVE MOST OF THE FAT FROM LOIN, THEN PLACE IN SMALL ROASTING PAN. MIX FLOUR, SALT, SUGAR, MUSTARD AND PEPPER, RUB MIXTURE ALL OVER ROAST. ADD THE ONION, SPRINKLE CARAWAY SEED ON TOP, POUR IN WATER AND COVER. COOK AT 325° FOR 2 HOURS OR UNTIL WELL DONE. SLICE COOKED PORK, AND POUR SAUCE OVER. SERVE WITH THE RED CABBAGE SALAD PAGE 83 AND WHIPPED POTATOES.

SERVES 8

# Holubtsi

2 CUPS SHORT-GRAIN RICE
1 TSP. SALT
1 ONION, DICED
4 TBSP. BUTTER
8 SLICES BACK BACON, FINELY CUT
½ TSP. SALT
¼ TSP. PEPPER
1 HEAD WINTER CABBAGE

RINSE RICE LIGHTLY, COVER WITH COLD WATER TO ½" ABOVE RICE. ADD 1 TSP. SALT, BRING TO A BOIL, STIR, COVER AND SIMMER 10 MINUTES. WHILE RICE IS COOKING FRY ONION IN 1½ TBSP. BUTTER UNTIL JUST TENDER. TO THE PARTLY COOKED RICE ADD ONION, BACON, 1 TBSP. BUTTER, SALT AND PEPPER. MIX WELL.

CONTINUED

A FEW DAYS BEFORE MAKING CABBAGE ROLLS I REMOVE THE CORE AND OUTER LEAVES, WRAP IN FOIL AND FREEZE. THAW OVERNIGHT AT ROOM TEMPERATURE. REMOVE LEAVES CAREFULLY, CUT OFF RIB, CUT LEAF IN PIECES LARGE ENOUGH TO HOLD 1 TBSP. FILLING. PLACE LEAF IN PALM OF HAND, PUT 1 TBSP. FILLING TO ONE SIDE, ROLL UP LIGHTLY. TUCK IN ENDS AND ARRANGE IN LAYERS IN A BUTTERED CASSEROLE DISH. SPRINKLE EACH LAYER WITH SALT AND PEPPER. FILL TO 1" FROM TOP, DAB WITH BUTTER OR LAY A COUPLE SLICES OF BACON ON TOP. WHEN READY TO COOK, ADD ½ CUP WATER, COVER AND BAKE IN 325° OVEN ABOUT 2½ HOURS. SERVE WITH A SIDE DISH OF SOUR CREAM.

SERVES 4-6

# Varenyky

| 2 CUPS | FLOUR |
|---|---|
| 1 TSP. | SALT |
| 1/2 CUP | COLD MASHED POTATOES |
| 2 | EGG YOLKS |
| 1 TBSP. | MELTED LARD, COOLED |
| 1/2 CUP | COLD WATER |

IN A LARGE BOWL MIX FLOUR, SALT AND POTATOES AS YOU WOULD PASTRY TO BLEND IN POTATOES. BEAT EGG YOLKS, ADD MELTED LARD AND WATER. MIX, THEN POUR OVER FLOUR MIXTURE. MIX WITH A FORK, THEN WITH HANDS. YOU MAY ADD MORE FLOUR OR WATER, IF NEEDED. TURN OUT ONTO COUNTER AND KNEAD LIKE BREAD UNTIL SMOOTH. COVER WITH MIXING BOWL AND LET REST FOR 30 MINUTES. WITH A SHARP KNIFE CUT IN HALF AND ROLL OUT ONTO FLOURED COUNTER TO ALMOST PAPER THIN. CUT CIRCLES 2½" IN DIAMETER.

CONTINUED

HOLDING 1 CIRCLE IN PALM OF HAND PLACE A GOOD TEASPOON OF FILLING* IN CENTER. FOLD DOUGH OVER AND PINCH EDGES TOGETHER FIRMLY, TO SEAL. PLACE FILLED PYROHY ON A LIGHTLY FLOURED SURFACE UNTIL ALL ARE FINISHED. USE A LARGE POT. FILL WITH BOILING WATER AND ALLOW IT TO REACH A ROLLING BOIL. GENTLY DROP PYROHY IN, ABOUT 12 AT A TIME. STIR CAREFULLY. WHEN THEY ALL RISE TO THE TOP REDUCE HEAT AND COOK UNTIL PUFFY, 3 TO 4 MINUTES. REMOVE, DRAIN AND PLACE IN A LARGE BUTTERED BAKING DISH, SPRINKLE WITH ONION-BACON MIXTURE * COVER AND PLACE IN A PREHEATED 300° OVEN FOR 10 MINUTES.

* NOTE :    RECIPE ON FOLLOWING PAGES.

MAKES 48

# Varenyky Fillings

| | |
|---|---|
| 2 CUPS | HOT MASHED POTATOES |
| 1/2 | ONION, FINELY DICED |
| 1 TBSP. | BUTTER |
| 1 CUP | GRATED CHEDDAR CHEESE |
| 1/2 TSP. | SALT |
| 1/4 TSP. | PEPPER |

PEEL 4 POTATOES, QUARTER, BOIL IN SALTED WATER UNTIL VERY TENDER. DRAIN AND MASH VERY WELL. FRY ONION IN BUTTER UNTIL SOFT AND TRANSPARENT. GRATE CHEESE; WHILE POTATOES ARE STILL HOT ADD CHEESE AND ONION. WHIP TOGETHER TO MELT CHEESE AND BLEND. ADD SALT AND PEPPER, MORE SEASONING MAY BE REQUIRED AS SOME FLAVOR IS LOST DURING COOKING. ALLOW TO COOL BEFORE USING.

NOTE: PYROHY ARE GREAT FRIED THE NEXT DAY.

MAKES 48

# Varenyky Dressing

| | |
|---|---|
| 5 | SLICES BACON |
| 1 | ONION |
| ½ CUP | MARGARINE |
| | SOUR CREAM |

CUT UP BACON FINELY, FRY. CHOP ONION AND ADD WHEN BACON IS HALF COOKED. FRY UNTIL ONION IS TENDER, THEN ADD THE MARGARINE AND ALLOW IT TO MELT. AS THE PYROHY IS BAKING, SPRINKLE DRESSING OVER TOP TO COAT PYROHY SO THEY WON'T STICK TOGETHER. IT ALSO ENHANCES THE FLAVOR. HAVE PLENTY OF SOUR CREAM IN A SIDE DISH SO GUESTS MAY HELP THEMSELVES.

NOTE: VARENYKY WILL ALSO FREEZE WELL, EITHER RAW OR COOKED. NEVER THAW BEFORE COOKING.

# CRUNCHY DILL PICKLES

20 LBS. CUCUMBERS
8 HEADS DILL
2 TSP. ALUM
8 LARGE CLOVES GARLIC
3 QTS. WATER
7 CUPS VINEGAR
7/8 CUP COARSE PICKLING SALT

ALWAYS USE FRESH DARK GREEN CUCUMBERS WITH A ROUGH SKIN, NOT MORE THAN 3" TO 4" LONG. WASH THOROUGHLY, PLACE IN A LARGE CONTAINER, COVER WITH COLD WATER AND LET SIT AT LEAST FOR 12 HOURS. A FOAM MAY APPEAR BUT DON'T WORRY ABOUT IT. RINSE CUCUMBERS IN CLEAN COLD WATER AND PACK INTO STERILIZED QUART JARS. TO EACH JAR ADD 1 HEAD DILL, 1/4 TSP. ALUM, AND A LARGE CLOVE GARLIC, QUARTERED.

CONTINUED

BOIL WATER, VINEGAR AND
SALT UNTIL SALT HAS DISSOLVED,
THEN POUR OVER CUCUMBERS IN
JARS. FILL TO TOP WITH BRINE.
LET SIT FOR 3 WEEKS BEFORE YOU
EAT THEM.

NOTE : I PREFER CUCUMBERS
FROM B.C. AND ALSO FOUND THAT
ONTARIO HAS AN EXCELLENT
CLIMATE FOR CUCUMBERS.
YOU DON'T NEED NEW
LIDS FOR PICKLES; I ALWAYS USE OLD
ONES. BE SURE TO STERILIZE.
IF YOU LIKE A PICKLE
THAT BITES YOU BACK, PUT 1 HOT
RED PEPPER IN JAR.

MAKES 8 QTS.

# Sauerkraut

20 LBS. WINTER CABBAGE
½ LB. COARSE PICKLING SALT
       BLACK PEPPERCORNS

REMOVE OUTER LEAVES, QUARTER, CORE AND PLACE IN ICE WATER UNTIL ALL ARE PREPARED. DRAIN AND SHRED VERY FINE. PLACE A 4" LAYER OF CABBAGE IN BOTTOM OF 5 GALLON CROCK, SPRINKLE WITH 1 TBSP. SALT AND 5 PEPPERCORNS. REPEAT LAYERS UNTIL ALL CABBAGE HAS BEEN USED. MIX WELL WITH HANDS, THEN PRESS DOWN FIRMLY. COVER COMPLETELY WITH A PIECE OF DAMP CHEESECLOTH, A PLATE, AND A 10 LB. WEIGHT. COVER CROCK WITH A TEA TOWEL AND STORE AT 65°F.

CONTINUED

AFTER 2 WEEKS CHECK FOR FERMENTATION; A SCUM WILL FORM. ONCE FERMENTATION STARTS YOU WILL NEED TO WASH CLOTH AND PLATE EVERY DAY OR TWO. LEAVE IN CROCK FOR AT LEAST 6 WEEKS UNTIL FERMENTATION HAS BEEN COMPLETED. THEN PACK LOOSELY IN STERILIZED PINT JARS. FILL WITH BRINE FROM CROCK AND SEAL. STORE IN A COOL PLACE. IF YOU DON'T HAVE ENOUGH BRINE MIX 2 TBSP. COARSE PICKLING SALT TO 1 QUART WATER. BRING TO A BOIL, THEN COOL BEFORE USING.

NOTE: TO MAKE SOUR HEADS FOR CABBAGE ROLLS, USE SAME PROCEDURE, PLACE 3 HEADS IN WITH SAUERKRAUT. PACK IN QUART JARS, COVER WITH BRINE AND SEAL. PLACE JARS TOP DOWN IN 1/2" OF WATER OVER MEDIUM HEAT FOR 5 MINUTES FOR A GOOD SEAL.

MAKES 20 QTS.

# Peking Duck

3½ LB.   DUCK
5  TSP.   SUGAR
3  TSP.   SALT
½  TSP.   MONOSODIUM GLUTAMATE
¼  CUP    BOILING WATER
1  TBSP.  LIQUID HONEY
5  DROPS  RED FOOD COLORING
3          CARROTS
3          GREEN ONIONS
32         CRÊPES  PG. 47
           HOISIN SAUCE

SPECIAL EQUIPMENT:
           BICYCLE PUMP AND NEEDLE
           HAIR DRYER
           HEAVY STRING
           TAPESTRY NEEDLE
           COARSE WHITE THREAD
           PASTRY BRUSH
           11" x 16" DRIP PAN
           WIRE RACK

CONTINUED

LEAVE DUCK IN WRAPPER AND DEFROST IN REFRIGERATOR OVERNIGHT, THEN WASH AND DRY DUCK THOROUGHLY WITH PAPER TOWEL. REMOVE ANY EXCESS FAT FROM INSIDE. TRIM EXTRA SKIN FROM NECK CAVITY, BEING SURE TO LEAVE ENOUGH SKIN SO THAT YOU CAN SEW UP NECK CAVITY NEATLY, FOLDING CUT EDGE UNDER 1/4". SEW SPOT ON TOP OF TAIL WHERE OIL SACK WAS REMOVED; SQUEEZE SKIN TOGETHER. CHECK DUCK FOR ANY OTHER BROKEN SKIN. PLACE MIXTURE OF SUGAR, SALT AND MONOSODIUM GLUTAMATE INSIDE CAVITY, THEN SEW UP SAME AS NECK CAVITY. SHAKE DUCK TO SPREAD MIXTURE INSIDE. TUCK WING TIPS UNDER WING ARMS. INSERT PUMP NEEDLE JUST UNDER THE SKIN ABOUT MIDDLE OF BACK AND PUMP IN AIR LIFTING SKIN UNTIL DUCK IS TWICE ORIGINAL SIZE. REMOVE NEEDLE, SEW UP HOLE.

CONTINUED

USING HEAVY STRING MAKE A HANGER AND LOOP AROUND WINGS, HANG DUCK. SET A SMALL BOWL BENEATH TO CATCH DRIPS. SET HAIR DRYER ON COOL AND BLOW-DRY SKIN COMPLETELY, ESPECIALLY UNDER WING ARMS. WHEN DUCK IS DRY AND LOOKS SHINY PAINT SKIN ALL OVER WITH MIXTURE OF WATER, HONEY AND FOOD COLORING. AGAIN DRY IN SAME MANNER. HEAT OVEN TO 350° WHEN HOT PLACE DRIP PAN ON BOTTOM SHELF WITH 2 CUPS WATER IN IT. LAY DUCK, BREAST DOWN, ON WIRE RACK, DON'T USE A ROASTING PAN. PLACE ON NEXT SHELF OF OVEN. COOK 40 MINUTES UNTIL A VERY RICH DARK BROWN, TURN AND BROWN BREAST SIDE. TOTAL COOKING TIME IS ABOUT 1½ HOURS.

CONTINUED

WHILE DUCK IS COOKING MAKE CRÊPES AND PREPARE THE VEGETABLES. SLICE CARROTS VERY THINLY AND 3" LONG, CUT GREEN ONIONS SAME LENGTH. DIVIDE THE CARROTS AND ONIONS ON 2 SMALL PLATES. PUT HOISIN SAUCE IN 2 SMALL BOWLS. ARRANGE CRÊPES ON 2 PLATTERS. ONCE DUCK HAS COOKED, CUT OFF SMALL PIECES OF SKIN AND MEAT, AND ARRANGE NEATLY ON 2 PLATES. TO SERVE, LET GUESTS PREPARE THEIR OWN BY SPREADING CRÊPE WITH HOISIN SAUCE, ADDING DUCK SKIN AND MEAT, A FEW SLIVERS OF CARROTS AND ONIONS. ROLL UP AND EAT USING FINGERS. THE CARCASS, WITH CHICKEN BACKS AND CHINESE MUSHROOMS MAKE A SOUP BROTH; TRADITIONALLY SERVED AT THE END OF THE MEAL. SPECIAL THANKS TO JOHN LEUNG FOR HIS ASSISTANCE AND EXPERTISE.

SERVES 8

# Chinese Mushroom Soup

| | | |
|---|---|---|
| 1 | | SMALL CHICKEN BREAST |
| 1 | TSP. | CORNSTARCH |
| 2 | TSP. | SHERRY |
| ½ | TSP. | SALT |
| 4 | | DRIED CHINESE MUSHROOMS |
| 4 | CUPS | CHICKEN STOCK |
| ¼ | CUP | BAMBOO SHOOTS, SLICED |
| 1 | | GREEN ONION, CHOPPED |

SLICE CHICKEN IN THIN STRIPS, THEN MARINATE IN MIXTURE OF CORNSTARCH, SHERRY AND SALT. SOAK MUSHROOMS IN WARM WATER FOR 15 MINUTES, THEN SLICE THINLY AND DISCARD STEMS. BRING CHICKEN STOCK, MUSHROOMS AND BAMBOO SHOOTS TO A BOIL, THEN SIMMER 5 MINUTES. ADD CHICKEN, STIR, REMOVE FROM HEAT, SPRINKLE WITH GREEN ONION AND SERVE.

SERVES 4

PEKING DUCK

PG. 134

# SHRIMP FRIED RICE

2 TBSP.  PEANUT OIL
1/2 TSP.  SALT
1/4 TSP.  GARLIC POWDER
2 CUPS  FINELY CUT SHRIMP
1/2 CUP  DICED ONION
1/2 CUP  DICED CELERY
1/2 CUP  DICED GREEN PEPPER
1/2 CUP  SLICED MUSHROOMS
1/4 CUP  CHOPPED WATER CHESTNUTS
4 CUPS  COOKED RICE
1 TBSP.  SOY SAUCE
3       EGGS
2 TBSP.  CHOPPED GREEN ONION

IN A LARGE ELECTRIC FRYING PAN HEAT OIL ON HIGH, ADD NEXT 8 INGREDIENTS. STIR-FRY 2 MINUTES, ADD RICE AND SOY SAUCE. TURN HEAT TO MEDIUM, MAKE ROOM IN CENTER, ADD EGGS. AS EGGS START TO SET, MIX IN WITH RICE. TURN HEAT TO WARM, COVER PAN UNTIL READY TO SERVE. CHICKEN, PORK OR BEEF MAY BE USED INSTEAD OF SHRIMP.

SERVES 8

# Shrimp Egg Rolls

| | | |
|---|---|---|
| 1 | CUP | CHOPPED COOKED SHRIMP |
| 1 | CUP | CHOPPED BEAN SPROUTS |
| 1 | CUP | MINCED CELERY |
| 1/2 | CUP | MINCED MUSHROOMS |
| 1/2 | CUP | MINCED WATER CHESTNUTS |
| 1 | TSP. | SOY SAUCE |
| 1 1/2 | TSP. | SALT |
| 1 | TSP. | SHERRY |
| 1 | TSP. | MONOSODIUM GLUTAMATE |
| 1/4 | TSP. | SUGAR |
| 1 | CUP | FLOUR |
| 1 | TSP. | SALT |
| 4 | | EGGS |
| 1 | CUP | WATER |
| | | OIL FOR FRYING |

CONTINUED

MIX FIRST 10 INGREDIENTS, BLEND WELL, CHILL IN REFRIGERATOR. FOR WRAPPERS COMBINE FLOUR, 1 TSP. SALT, 3 BEATEN EGGS. STIR IN WATER SLOWLY UNTIL A SMOOTH THIN BATTER IS FORMED. HEAT 6" FRYING PAN, OIL LIGHTLY, ADD 1 TBSP. BATTER, TIP TO SPREAD. COOK ONLY UNTIL SET, DO NOT TURN. LAY ON PAPER TOWEL, COOK REMAINING BATTER. DRAIN SHRIMP MIXTURE, PLACE 1 TBSP. ON EACH WRAPPER AND FOLD 2 SIDES OVER. BRUSH WRAPPER WITH 1 BEATEN EGG. PLACE SEAM SIDE DOWN ON COOKIE SHEET, AND REFRIGERATE UNCOVERED FOR 1 HOUR. HEAT 1" OIL IN FRYING PAN. FRY ROLLS UNTIL GOLDEN BROWN. MAY THEN BE FROZEN OR BAKED IN 400° OVEN FOR 10 MINUTES. SERVE WITH PLUM SAUCE OR HOT MUSTARD.

SERVES 16

# Curried Beef

| | | |
|---|---|---|
| 3/4 | LB. | ROUND STEAK |
| 1 | TSP. | SOY SAUCE |
| 1/2 | TSP. | SALT |
| 1/4 | TSP. | SUGAR |
| 1/2 | TSP. | CURRY POWDER |
| 1 | TSP. | GRATED FRESH GINGER |
| 1/4 | TSP. | CAYENNE |
| 1 | TSP. | SHERRY |
| 1/4 | TSP. | BAKING SODA |
| 1 | TBSP. | CORN STARCH |
| 1 | TSP. | PEANUT OIL |
| 2 | TBSP. | PEANUT OIL |
| 7 | OZ. | BABY CORN, SLICED |
| 2 | | GREEN ONIONS, 2" LENGTHS |
| 1 | TBSP. | CORNSTARCH |
| 1/4 | TSP. | HOT DRY MUSTARD |
| 1 | TSP. | CURRY POWDER |
| 3/4 | CUP | WATER |

CONTINUED

SLICE BEEF AS THINLY AS
YOU CAN. ADD NEXT 7 INGREDIENTS,
MIX WELL BY HAND. 20 MINUTES
BEFORE COOKING TIME ADD SODA,
MIX IN WELL. COAT WITH 1 TBSP.
CORNSTARCH, DRIZZLE WITH 1 TSP.
OIL. HEAT WOK, ADD OIL. STIR-FRY
BEEF 4 MINUTES, ADD CORN AND
ONIONS. COOK ANOTHER MINUTE
OR TWO, THEN REDUCE HEAT AND
THICKEN WITH MIXTURE OF
CORNSTARCH, MUSTARD, CURRY AND
WATER. COOK 1 MINUTE AND SERVE
WITH STEAMED RICE.

SERVES 4

# Beef In Oyster Sauce

| | | |
|---|---|---|
| 1 | LB. | FLANK STEAK |
| 2 | TBSP. | SHERRY |
| 1 | TBSP. | SOY SAUCE |
| 2 | TBSP. | OYSTER SAUCE |
| 1 | TBSP. | CORNSTARCH |
| 1 | | GREEN PEPPER |
| 1 | | SLICE FRESH GINGER |
| 2 | | GREEN ONIONS |
| 4 | TBSP. | PEANUT OIL |
| 1 | TSP. | SALT |

NOTE:

WHEN USING A CHEAPER CUT OF BEEF FOR CHINESE DISHES, MIX WITH BAKING SODA WHICH TENDERIZES THE MEAT. HOWEVER LEAVE ON ONLY 20 MINUTES BEFORE COOKING, AFTER WHICH BEEF WILL BECOME TOUGH.

CONTINUED

CUT BEEF ACROSS THE GRAIN IN THIN SLICES. MIX WITH NEXT 4 INGREDIENTS. MARINATE 1 HOUR. CUT GREEN PEPPER INTO 1" SQUARES. CUT GINGER INTO SLIVERS AND ONION IN 1" LENGTHS. HEAT WOK, ADD OIL, STIR-FRY BEEF 1 MINUTE. ADD GINGER, ONIONS AND GREEN PEPPER. ADD SALT, STIR-FRY ANOTHER 2 MINUTES, SERVE HOT.

SERVES 4

# BEEF AND BROCCOLI

| | | |
|---|---|---|
| 3/4 LB. | SIRLOIN STEAK | |
| 1 TSP. | SOY SAUCE | |
| 1/2 TSP. | SALT | |
| 1/2 TSP. | SUGAR | |
| 1 TSP. | SHERRY | |
| 1/2 TSP. | BAKING SODA | |
| 1 TBSP. | CORNSTARCH | |
| | PEANUT OIL | |
| 1 TBSP. | FERMENTED BLACK BEANS | |
| 1 CUP | HOT WATER | |
| 1 CLOVE | GARLIC, CRUSHED | |
| 1 TBSP. | CORNSTARCH | |
| | COLD WATER | |
| 2 HEADS BROCCOLI | | |

REMOVE FAT, SLICE STEAK VERY THINLY. PLACE SLICED MEAT IN A BOWL, ADD SOY SAUCE, SALT, SUGAR, SHERRY, MIX WELL AND LET MARINATE FOR 1 HOUR. 20 MINUTES BEFORE COOKING ADD BAKING SODA, CORNSTARCH AND DRIP 1 TSP. OIL. MIX WELL WITH HANDS.

CONTINUED

PUT BEANS IN A METAL BOWL AND CRUSH WITH A WOODEN MALLET. ADD HOT WATER, SET ASIDE. PEEL AND CRUSH GARLIC, MIX CORNSTARCH WITH ½ CUP COLD WATER, CUT BROCCOLI INTO FLORETS. RINSE BROCCOLI UNDER COLD WATER, DRAIN WELL. HEAT WOK OVER HIGH HEAT, ADD OIL AND BROCCOLI, STIR-FRY 2 MINUTES JUST TO COAT WITH OIL. ADD 1 TBSP. COLD WATER, COVER AND STEAM 3 MINUTES. REMOVE TO OVENPROOF DISH, SET IN WARM OVEN. CLEAN WOK, PLACE BACK ON HIGH HEAT, ADD 2 TBSP. OIL, CRUSHED GARLIC AND BEEF. STIR-FRY 5 MINUTES, REMOVE MEAT TO A BOWL, ADD BLACK BEANS AND CORNSTARCH. COOK UNTIL THICK WHILE STIRRING. ADD SALT TO TASTE. RETURN MEAT TO SAUCE LET SIMMER 3 MINUTES. ARRANGE BROCCOLI AROUND EDGE OF PLATTER, MOUND MEAT IN CENTER. A VERY ATTRACTIVE DISH WITH A CHINESE DINNER.

SERVES 4

149

# Chicken In Bird's Nest

| | | |
|---|---|---|
| 1 | | CHICKEN BREAST |
| 2 | TSP. | CORNSTARCH |
| 1 | TBSP. | WATER |
| 1 | | CARROT, 2" STRIPS |
| 1 | | ONION, SLICED |
| 1 | CUP | SLICED CHINESE CABBAGE |
| 2 | TBSP. | PEANUT OIL |
| 1 | TSP | WATER |
| 1 | PINCH | SALT |
| 1 | PINCH | SUGAR |
| 1 | PINCH | MONOSODIUM GLUTAMATE |
| ½ | TSP. | GINGER WINE, PG. 159 |
| ½ | CUP | CHICKEN STOCK |
| 1½ | TBSP. | OYSTER SAUCE |
| 2 | | POTATOES |
| ¼ | TSP. | SALT |
| 2 | TBSP. | CORNSTARCH |
| | | OIL FOR DEEP FRYING |
| | | LETTUCE FOR GARNISH |

CONTINUED

CUT CHICKEN INTO THIN STRIPS.
BLEND CORNSTARCH AND WATER,
WORK HALF INTO MEAT. PREPARE
CARROTS, ONION AND CABBAGE. HEAT
WOK, ADD 1 TBSP. OIL, STIR-FRY
CHICKEN FOR 2 MINUTES. REMOVE,
WIPE OUT WOK, HEAT AGAIN, ADD
1 TBSP. OIL, TOSS IN VEGETABLES.
STIR-FRY TO COAT WITH OIL, ADD
1 TSP. WATER, COVER, STEAM FOR
1 MINUTE. RETURN CHICKEN TO WOK,
ADD SEASONINGS, SHERRY, STOCK,
REMAINING CORNSTARCH MIXTURE
AND OYSTER SAUCE. BRING TO A
BOIL, SIMMER 1 MINUTE. TURN
INTO BIRD'S NEST. TO MAKE NEST,
PEEL POTATOES, CUT INTO THIN STRIPS.
RINSE AND DRY, SPRINKLE WITH SALT
AND CORNSTARCH. ARRANGE THE
SHREDS CRISS-CROSS BETWEEN 2-
6" STRAINERS. DEEP-FRY AT 375°
UNTIL GOLDEN BROWN. DRAIN,
LAY ON A BED OF LETTUCE, FILL.

SERVES 4

# Hot Singapore Chicken

| | |
|---|---|
| 1 | CHICKEN BREAST |
| 1/2 CUP | WATER CHESTNUTS |
| 1/2 CUP | BAMBOO SHOOTS |
| 1/2 CUP | PEAS |
| 1/2 CUP | WHITE SUGAR |
| 1/3 CUP | VINEGAR |
| 2/3 CUP | WATER |
| 1/4 CUP | TOMATO SAUCE |
| 1 TSP. | CAYENNE PEPPER |
| 1/8 TSP. | PAPRIKA |
| 1 TBSP. | CORNSTARCH |
| 1/4 CUP | WATER |
| 1 CUP | FLOUR |
| 1 CUP | BEER |
| 1/2 TSP. | SALT |
| 3 CUPS | PEANUT OIL |

CONTINUED

CUT CHICKEN, WATER CHESTNUTS, BAMBOO SHOOTS INTO 1/4" STRIPS. MEASURE PEAS. IN A SAUCEPAN COMBINE NEXT 6 ITEMS. BRING TO A BOIL, THICKEN WITH CORNSTARCH AND 1/4 CUP WATER, SIMMER 5 MINUTES. MIX FLOUR BEER AND SALT TO BATTER THE CHICKEN. COOK A FEW STRIPS AT A TIME IN WOK WITH OIL. FRY UNTIL GOLDEN BROWN, DRAIN. EMPTY OIL, EXCEPT 1 TSP. ADD VEGETABLES, STIR-FRY 4 MINUTES. ADD SAUCE, AND CHICKEN. MIX TO COAT CHICKEN COMPLETELY WITH SAUCE. THIS SAUCE IS VERY HOT, SO I WOULD SUGGEST YOU START WITH 1/4 TSP. CAYENNE.

SERVES 4

# Sweet And Sour Spareribs

3 LBS.    PORK SPARERIBS, 2" LENGTH
1 TSP.    ACCENT
1 TSP.    SUGAR
½ TSP.    PEPPER
1 CLOVE   GARLIC, CRUSHED
½ CUP     SOY SAUCE
2 TBSP.   MAZOLA OIL
½ CUP     FLOUR
1½ CUPS.  BROWN SUGAR
3/4 CUP   WHITE VINEGAR
1¼ CUPS   WATER
1 TBSP.   CORNSTARCH
¼ CUP     WATER

CONTINUED

WASH AND DRY SPARERIBS, REMOVE EXCESS FAT AND CUT INTO INDIVIDUAL PIECES. MIX NEXT 5 ITEMS IN A LARGE BOWL. ADD RIBS, MIX TO COAT, MARINATE 2 HOURS, STIR A FEW TIMES. HEAT OVEN TO 325°, PUT OIL IN ENAMEL ROASTER. COAT RIBS IN FLOUR, PLACE IN ROASTER, BAKE 1½ HOURS. STIR A COUPLE TIMES WHILE COOKING. TO MAKE SAUCE, COMBINE SUGAR, VINEGAR AND WATER IN SAUCEPAN. STIR TO DISSOLVE SUGAR, BRING TO A BOIL, THICKEN WITH CORNSTARCH MIXED WITH ¼ CUP WATER. COOK UNTIL CLEAR. ADD RIBS, DRAIN OFF GREASE. SIMMER 15 MINUTES. SERVE WITH STEAMED RICE AND A SALAD.

SERVES 4

# Chinese Barbecued Pork

| 2 LB. | PORK SHOULDER |
|---|---|
| 2 TSP. | CHINESE FIVE SPICES POWDER |
| 1/4 TSP. | SUGAR |
| 1 TBSP. | DRY WHITE WINE |
| 1 TBSP. | SOY SAUCE |
| | RED FOOD COLORING |
| 1 TSP. | LIQUID HONEY |
| 1/2 TSP. | HOT WATER |

REMOVE FAT FROM PORK, MIX PORK WITH NEXT 4 INGREDIENTS. WORK WELL INTO PORK. ADD A FEW DROPS FOOD COLORING, RUB ALL OVER. COVER, LEAVE IN REFRIGERATOR OVERNIGHT. PLACE ON RACK ON COOKIE SHEET, ON CENTER OVEN RACK, WITH PAN OF WATER BELOW. BAKE ABOUT 1 1/2 HOURS AT 325°. GLAZE WITH HONEY AND WATER, A FEW MINUTES BEFORE ROAST IS DONE. REMOVE FROM OVEN, LET STAND 10 MINUTES. SLICE THINLY. SERVE AS AN ADDITIONAL DISH WITH A CHINESE DINNER.

SERVES 8

# CRAB FU YUNG

2-12 OZ. CRABS
1 TBSP.　GINGER WINE *
　　　　　PEANUT OIL
1　　　　 GREEN ONION, FINELY CHOPPED
1 TBSP.　FRESH GINGER, SHREDDED
2 TSP.　 SHERRY
2　　　　 EGGS, BEATEN

## SEASONING SAUCE:
1/4 CUP　CHICKEN STOCK
1 TSP.　 SALT
1/4 TSP.　MONOSODIUM GLUTAMATE
1/4 TSP.　PEPPER
1/2 TSP.　SESAME SEED OIL
1 TSP.　 CORNSTARCH

* TO MAKE GINGER WINE, HEAT 1/2 CUP SHERRY, ADD 2 TBSP. GRATED FRESH GINGER. SET ASIDE FOR 1 HOUR TO BLEND FLAVORS. KEEPS WELL IN A COVERED JAR IN REFRIGERATOR.

CONTINUED

159

BUY LIVE CRABS. PLUNGE
HEAD FIRST INTO A POT OF BOILING
WATER. BRING WATER BACK TO A
BOIL AND SIMMER 20 MINUTES. WASH
THOROUGHLY UNDER COLD RUNNING
WATER. REMOVE BACK SHELL AND
ALL INEDIBLE PARTS AND WASH.
CUT CRAB INTO LARGE PIECES.
PLACE IN A BOWL, SPRINKLE WITH
GINGER WINE. LEAVE SIT FOR
20 MINUTES.

NOTE :
YOU MUST USE LIVE
CRABS BECAUSE FROZEN CRAB
LOSES ITS' FLAVOR AND CRAB
MEAT WITHOUT A SHELL FALLS
APART.

CONTINUED

160

IN A SMALL BOWL MIX
STOCK, SALT, MONOSODIUM
GLUTAMATE, PEPPER, SESAME OIL,
CORNSTARCH. PUT 1/3 CUP OIL IN
HOT WOK, STIR-FRY CRAB FOR
2 MINUTES. REMOVE TO PLATTER,
DRAIN OFF OIL, ADD ONION, GINGER
AND SHERRY. COOK 1 MINUTE, ADD
CRAB AND SEASONING SAUCE.
SIMMER 2 MINUTES, POUR IN
WELL-BEATEN EGGS AND COOK
UNTIL JUST SET. STIR AND SERVE
ON A LARGE PLATTER. GIVE YOUR
GUESTS LONG-HANDLED FONDUE
FORKS TO REMOVE MEAT FROM
SHELLS.

SERVES 6

# NOTES

# DESSERTS AND DRINKS

# Cheese Cake

### CRUMB CRUST:
1 3/4 CUPS GRAHAM WAFER CRUMBS
1/4 CUP FINELY CHOPPED WALNUTS
1/2 TSP. CINNAMON
1/2 CUP MELTED BUTTER

### FILLING:
3        EGGS, BEATEN
16 OZ.    CREAM CHEESE, SOFT
1 CUP    WHITE SUGAR
1/4 TSP.   SALT
2 TSP.    VANILLA
1/2 TSP.   ALMOND EXTRACT
3 CUPS DAIRY SOUR CREAM

CONTINUED

FOR CRUST, COMBINE ALL INGREDIENTS. RESERVE 3 TBSP. FOR TOP; PRESS REMAINDER ON BOTTOM AND 2½" UP SIDES OF GREASED 9" SPRINGFORM PAN. TO MAKE FILLING, COMBINE ALL FILLING INGREDIENTS EXCEPT SOUR CREAM. BEAT SMOOTH BLEND IN SOUR CREAM. POUR INTO CRUST, TRIM WITH RESERVED CRUMBS. BAKE IN 350° OVEN, 40 MINUTES UNTIL JUST SET. FILLING WILL BE SOFT. COOL WELL, THEN CHILL IN REFRIGERATOR 4 TO 5 HOURS. TO SERVE, SLICE IN WEDGES. MAY BE DECORATED WITH STRAWBERRIES.

SERVES 20

# Black Forest Cake

1 PKG.  DEVIL'S FOOD CAKE MIX
½ CUP  KIRSCH
        FILLING (SEE BELOW)*
2 CUPS  PITTED BLACK CHERRIES,
        QUARTERED
2 CUPS  WHIPPING CREAM
1 TBSP.  SUGAR
½ TSP.  VANILLA
1 TBSP.  KIRSCH
        CHOCOLATE CURLS
        MARASCHINO CHERRIES

        MAKE CAKE MIX ACCORDING
TO PACKAGE DIRECTIONS AND
DIVIDE EVENLY INTO 4 GREASED
9" ROUND CAKE PANS. BAKE AT 325°
FOR 25 MINUTES. COOL WELL.
SPRINKLE ALL ½ CUP OF KIRSCH
EQUALLY OVER THE 4 LAYERS.

CONTINUED

PLACE 1 LAYER ON CAKE
PLATE ; SPREAD 1/3 FILLING ON TOP.
PRESS 1/3 CHERRIES INTO FILLING. TOP
WITH SECOND LAYER. REPEAT TWICE
PLACING TOP LAYER ON FIRMLY. JUST
BEFORE SERVING, WHIP CREAM, ADD
SUGAR, VANILLA AND KIRSCH. SPREAD
OVER TOP AND SIDES OF CAKE.
DECORATE WITH CHOCOLATE CURLS,
SURROUND WITH MARASCHINO
CHERRIES.

* BUTTER CREAM FILLING:
1/2 CUP    SOFT BUTTER
1  TSP.    STRONG COFFEE
           PINCH OF SALT
3 1/2 CUPS ICING SUGAR
2  TBSP.   CREAM

CREAM BUTTER, BEAT IN
SALT AND COFFEE, THEN SUGAR. ADD
CREAM TO REACH A HEAVY SPREADING
CONSISTENCY. USE A POTATO
PEELER FOR CHOCOLATE CURLS.

SERVES 12

167

# New York Squares

FIRST LAYER:
1/2 CUP   BUTTER
1/4 CUP   BROWN SUGAR
1/3 CUP   COCOA
1/2 TSP.  VANILLA
1         EGG
2 CUPS    GRAHAM WAFER CRUMBS
1 CUP     COCONUT
1/2 CUP   FINELY CHOPPED WALNUTS

MELT BUTTER IN SAUCEPAN, BLEND IN REMAINING INGREDIENTS IN ORDER GIVEN. MIX WELL, THEN PRESS INTO 13"x8" GREASED PAN. MAKE NEXT LAYER.

CONTINUED

## SECOND LAYER:

1 CUP BUTTER
4 TBSP. VANILLA PUDDING POWDER
4 TBSP. MILK
4 CUPS ICING SUGAR
6 OZ. SEMI-SWEET CHOCOLATE
1½ TBSP. BUTTER

CREAM BUTTER, BLEND IN PUDDING POWDER, THEN ADD 1 TBSP. MILK AND 1 CUP ICING SUGAR. MIX WELL; CONTINUE ADDING 1 TBSP. MILK AND 1 CUP SUGAR EACH TIME UNTIL ALL IS USED. SPREAD OVER FIRST LAYER. CHILL 1 HOUR. MELT CHOCOLATE WITH BUTTER IN SAUCEPAN OVER HOT WATER. BLEND, THEN SPREAD OVER CHILLED LAYERS. DO NOT RETURN TO REFRIGERATOR LET CHOCOLATE SET, THEN CUT INTO 1" x 1" SQUARES.

MAKES 104 SQ.

# Chocolate Rum Balls

1¾ CUPS GRAHAM WAFER CRUMBS
1   CUP   FINELY GROUND PECANS
1   CUP   ICING SUGAR
¼ CUP   COCOA
3 TBSP.  CORN SYRUP
¼ CUP   DARK RUM
           ICING SUGAR

COMBINE ALL INGREDIENTS WELL. IF MIXTURE APPEARS DRY, ADD A BIT MORE SYRUP. SHAPE INTO 1" BALLS AND DREDGE IN ICING SUGAR. STORE IN TIGHTLY COVERED CONTAINER TO PREVENT DRYING.

MAKES 36

170

# PINEAPPLE SQUARES

2½ CUPS GRAHAM WAFER CRUMBS
½ CUP BUTTER, MELTED
½ CUP BUTTER
1½ CUPS ICING SUGAR
2 EGGS
14 OZ. CRUSHED PINEAPPLE, DRAIN
½ PINT WHIPPING CREAM, WHIPPED

SET ASIDE ¼ CUP CRUMBS, ADD MELTED BUTTER TO REST AND PRESS INTO 8"x8" GREASED BAKING PAN. BAKE 15 MINUTES AT 325°. COOL. CREAM BUTTER, ADD ICING SUGAR AND EGGS, BLEND WITH MIXER UNTIL LIGHT. SPREAD ON CRUST. FOLD PINEAPPLE INTO WHIPPED CREAM AND SPREAD OVER FIRST FILLING. SPRINKLE ¼ CUP CRUMBS OVER TOP. REFRIGERATE 4 HOURS. CUT INTO 12 SQUARES. THIS IS A LOVELY LIGHT DESSERT.

MAKES 12 SQ.

# Peach Crêpes

CRÊPES:
½ CUP   MILK
1        EGG
1 TSP.   COGNAC
1 TSP.   BUTTER, MELTED
½ TSP.   VANILLA
½ CUP   FLOUR
1 TBSP. BERRY SUGAR
1 PINCH SALT

PLACE ALL INGREDIENTS IN A BLENDER ON MEDIUM SPEED FOR 2 TO 3 MINUTES UNTIL WELL BLENDED. LET BATTER REST IN REFRIGERATOR 2 HOURS. MAKE 8 CRÊPES USING METHOD ON PG. 47

CONTINUED

## PEACH FILLING:

3 TBSP. BUTTER
6 TBSP. BERRY SUGAR
1/2 CUP WHIPPING CREAM, WHIPPED
2 CUPS DRAINED PEACHES
GRANULATED SUGAR
2 TBSP. COGNAC

CREAM BUTTER AND BERRY SUGAR. DIVIDE EVENLY, SPREAD OVER CRÊPES. FOLD WELL-DRAINED PEACHES INTO WHIPPED CREAM; DIVIDE EVENLY OVER BUTTER-SUGAR SPREAD CRÊPES. ROLL UP, PLACE SEAM SIDE DOWN IN GREASED SHALLOW BAKING DISH. SPRINKLE LIGHTLY WITH GRANULATED SUGAR AND THE COGNAC. BAKE IN 375° OVEN 5 TO 8 MINUTES UNTIL SUGAR MELTS AND CRÊPES ARE WARMED THROUGH.

SERVES 4

# Amaretto Apple Crisp

| 6 | APPLES, PARED |
|---|---|
| 1/4 CUP | SUGAR |
| 1/2 TSP. | CINNAMON |
| 2 TBSP. | AMARETTO |
| 1/4 CUP | BUTTER |
| 1/2 CUP | FLOUR |
| 3/4 CUP | BROWN SUGAR |
| 1 TSP. | CINNAMON |

SLICE APPLES INTO 8"x 8" BUTTERED CAKE PAN. SPRINKLE WITH SUGAR, CINNAMON AND AMARETTO. MAKE CRUMBS OF REST OF INGREDIENTS AS YOU WOULD PASTRY AND SPRINKLE OVER APPLES. BAKE 30 MINUTES AT 350° UNTIL GOLDEN BROWN. SERVE WARM WITH ICE CREAM.

SERVES 8

# Cherry Delight

MAKE GRAHAM WAFER CRUST, PG. 64 PRESS ON THE BOTTOM AND SIDES OF 9" PIE PAN. BAKE IN 350° OVEN 15 MINUTES. COOL AND FILL.

FILLING:
| | | |
|---|---|---|
| 4 | OZ. | CREAM CHEESE, SOFTENED |
| ½ | CUP | BERRY SUGAR |
| ½ | TSP. | VANILLA |
| ⅛ | TSP. | SALT |
| ½ | PINT | WHIPPING CREAM |
| 19 | OZ. | CHERRY PIE FILLING |

COMBINE CHEESE, SUGAR, VANILLA AND SALT. MIX INTO A SMOOTH PASTE. WHIP CREAM AND LIGHTLY FOLD INTO CHEESE MIXTURE. POUR INTO CRUMB CRUST, SET IN REFRIGERATOR 8 TO 12 HOURS. CUT INTO WEDGES, SPOON ON TOPPING AND SERVE. THANKS TO PAULIE RICHARDSON, YELLOWKNIFE, N.W.T.

SERVES 6

# Caesars

48 OZ. CLAMATO JUICE
9 OZ. VODKA
1 TSP. WORCESTERSHIRE SAUCE
2 TBSP. LEMON JUICE
6 DROPS TABASCO SAUCE
1/4 TSP. SALT
1/8 TSP. PEPPER
1 SLICE LEMON
2 TBSP. LAWRY'S SEASONED SALT
2 CELERY STALKS

MIX FIRST 7 INGREDIENTS IN A TALL PITCHER. SET IN REFRIGERATOR TO CHILL. AT SERVING TIME USE 10 OZ. STEMMED GLASSES. FROST BY CUTTING A SPLIT IN THE LEMON, RUN IT AROUND THE RIM OF GLASS, DIP WET RIM IN SEASONED SALT. FILL GLASS HALFWAY WITH CRUSHED ICE, FILL WITH CAESAR MIX; ADD A NARROW STICK OF CELERY.

SERVES 6

# BULL SHOOTER

1¼  OZ.  VODKA
4  DROPS WORCESTERSHIRE SAUCE
¼  OZ.  LEMON JUICE
6  OZ.  BEEF BOUILLON
        SALT
        PEPPER

USE AN OLD FASHION GLASS WITH ICE CUBES. ADD VODKA, WORCESTERSHIRE SAUCE, LEMON JUICE. FILL GLASS WITH BEEF BOUILLON, ADD SALT AND PEPPER TO TASTE. STIR AND SERVE. THIS IS A GREAT DRINK FOR THE NEXT MORNING, IF YOU HAD 1 TOO MANY THE NIGHT BEFORE.

SERVES 1

179

# After Dinner Drinks

### GOLDEN CADILLAC
| | | |
|---|---|---|
| 1 | OZ. | GALLIANO |
| 1 | OZ. | MILK |
| 1 | OZ. | WHITE CRÈME DE CACAO |

SHAKE WELL WITH CRUSHED ICE AND STRAIN INTO CHAMPAGNE SHELL.

SERVES 1

### PINK SQUIRREL
| | | |
|---|---|---|
| 1 | OZ. | AMARETTO |
| ½ | OZ. | WHITE CRÈME DE CACAO |
| 1 | OZ. | MILK |
| ¼ | OZ. | GRENADINE |

SHAKE WELL WITH CRUSHED ICE AND STRAIN INTO A COCKTAIL GLASS.

SERVES 1

## GREEN LADY

3/4 OZ. GREEN CRÈME DE MENTHE
1/2 OZ. CHERRY BRANDY
3/4 OZ. MILK
1 GREEN CHERRY

SHAKE WELL WITH CRUSHED ICE AND STRAIN INTO A COCKTAIL GLASS. DECORATE WITH A GREEN CHERRY.
SERVES 1

## MEXICAN GRASSHOPPER

1 OZ. KAHLUA
1 OZ. GREEN CRÈME DE MENTHE
1 OZ. CEREAL CREAM

SHAKE WELL WITH CRUSHED ICE AND STRAIN INTO A COCKTAIL GLASS; WITH SHORT STRAWS.
SERVES 1

# Spanish Coffee

| 1 | PKG. | DREAM WHIP, 1/4 CUP MILK |
| | | SLICE OF LEMON |
| | | BERRY SUGAR |
| 6 | OZ. | DRAMBUIE |
| 1 | POT | EXTRA STRONG COFFEE |
| 2 | OZ. | TIA MARIA |

MIX DREAM WHIP WITH ONLY 1/4 CUP MILK. FROST GLASSES BY CUTTING A SPLIT IN LEMON, RUN AROUND RIM OF GLASS, THEN DIP RIM IN SUGAR. FOR EACH GLASS ADD 1 1/2 OZ. DRAMBUIE. FLAME, TILT GLASS WHILE TURNING TO MELT SUGAR A BIT. POUR IN HOT COFFEE TO 1" FROM TOP, ADD A SCOOP OF DREAM WHIP, POUR 1/2 OZ. TIA MARIA OVER, WRAP GLASS IN A NAPKIN AND SERVE.

SERVES 4

# POUCH DE CRÈME

8 LARGE EGGS
15 OZ.    CONDENSED MILK
12 OZ.    EVAPORATED MILK
1 TSP.    VANILLA
1 TSP.    ALMOND EXTRACT
1 TSP.    ANGOSTURA BITTERS
26 OZ.    WHITE RUM

　　　USE A LARGE BOWL, BEAT EGGS,
ADD MILK AND FLAVORINGS, MIX WELL.
ADD RUM STIR AND BOTTLE. LET SIT
4 DAYS BEFORE DRINKING. KEEP
REFRIGERATED. DONATED BY LISA
DILWORTH.

　　　　　　MAKES 3 QTS.

# NOTES

# INDEX

FRENCH ONION SOUP 77
MANHATTEN CLAM CHOWDER 75
MIZERIA OF CUCUMBERS 81
MUSHROOM CHEESE SALAD 84
ORIENTAL SPINACH SALAD 80
RED CABBAGE SALAD 83
SAUERKRAUT SALAD 85
SAUERKRAUT SOUP 78

ENTRÉES 89
ATLANTIC LOBSTER 90
BEEF WELLINGTON 102-103
BLACK PEPPERCORN STEAK 107
CURRIED CHICKEN WINGS 99
FLAMBÉED SHRIMP 96
MUSHROOM RICE 97
ORIENTAL CORNISH HENS 98
ORIENTAL STEAMED TROUT 94
PACIFIC COAST SALMON 95
POLYNESIAN CHICKEN 100-101
PORK STROGANOFF 104
SOLE IN WINE SAUCE 92-93
WHITEFISH ALMONDINE 91

# METRIC CONVERSION

| | | | |
|---|---|---|---|
| 1/4 | TSP. | 1 | ML |
| 1/2 | TSP. | 2 | ML |
| 3/4 | TSP. | 4 | ML |
| 1 | TSP. | 5 | ML |
| | | | |
| 1 | TBSP. | 15 | ML |
| 2 | TBSP. | 25 | ML |
| 3 | TBSP. | 50 | ML |
| | | | |
| 1/4 | CUP | 50 | ML |
| 1/3 | CUP | 75 | ML |
| 1/2 | CUP | 125 | ML |
| 2/3 | CUP | 150 | ML |
| 3/4 | CUP | 175 | ML |
| 1 | CUP | 250 | ML |
| | | | |
| 1 | OZ. | 25 | GRAMS |
| 1/4 | LB. | 125 | GRAMS |
| 1/2 | LB. | 250 | GRAMS |
| 3/4 | LB. | 350 | GRAMS |
| 1 | LB. | 500 | GRAMS |
| 1 1/2 | LB. | 700 | GRAMS |
| 2 | LB. | 1 | KG. |

## A GIFT WITH A TOUCH OF CLASS

PLEASE SEND _____ COPIES OF "COOKING WITH A TOUCH OF CLASS" $12.95 EACH, PLUS $1.50 TOTAL POSTAGE

NAME: _____

ADDRESS: _____

_____ POSTAL CODE: _____

CHEQUE OR MONEY ORDER PAYABLE TO: QUARREL PUBLISHING. INC. BOX 581  MIDNAPORE, ALBERTA CANADA    TOL 1J0

## A GIFT WITH A TOUCH OF CLASS

PLEASE SEND _____ COPIES OF "COOKING WITH A TOUCH OF CLASS" $12.95 EACH, PLUS $1.50 TOTAL POSTAGE

NAME: _____

ADDRESS: _____

_____ POSTAL CODE: _____

CHEQUE OR MONEY ORDER PAYABLE TO: QUARREL PUBLISHING INC. BOX 581 MIDNAPORE, ALBERTA CANADA    TOL 1J0